Acknowledgments

• • • • • • • • • • • • • • • • •

Although the process of writing a book may seem solitary at first glance, it is in fact a highly interconnected journey in which one relies constantly on the wisdom and input of others, both past and present. Over the years, I have been fortunate to be supported and buoyed by countless individuals both in my personal and professional worlds. There are indeed more people whom I will be forever indebted to than space permits, but I would like to highlight a handful of individuals whose encouragement, guidance, and understanding helped me immensely over the course of writing this book.

On a personal level, I would like to acknowledge my beautiful, talented, and brilliant wife, Kelly Paquette. You inspire me daily, and there is no one with whom I'd rather share life's adventures than you.

I would also like to thank my brother Gabriel Paquette, and my sister-in-law Johanna Richlin. Even though we are separated by thousands of miles, you are always close to my heart. And to my parents, Gregory and Kathy Paquette, thank you for your incredible generosity and kindness, and for helping me to always feel loved.

In my professional life, I have been inspired by countless colleagues who have helped guide me over the years. Though they are too many to list, I would like to identify a handful who have been integral to my work in recent years, including Kathryn Wetzler, Lisa Kuhlman, Laurie Wilson, Mitch Houston, Patricia Eaton, Julie Runkle, Rich Simon, Gil Levin, and Linda Graham.

Finally, to my incredible team at PESI Publishing, particularly Hillary Jenness, Linda Jackson, and Karsyn Morse. Thank you for taking a chance on me when I was a complete unknown, and for being such a wonderful partner in the journey of writing and publishing.

the
Happiness
toolbox

**56 Practices to Find Happiness,
Purpose & Productivity in Love, Work and Life**

Jonah Paquette, Psy.D.

Published by:
PESI Publishing & Media
PESI, Inc.
3839 White Ave.
Eau Claire, WI 54703

Cover Design: Amy Rubenzer
Editing By: Amy Farrar & Michelle Nelson
Layout: Mayfly Designs

Printed in the United States of America
ISBN: 9781683731290

PESI
Publishing
& Media
www.pesipublishing.com

Praise for *The Happiness Toolbox*

"Many books promise paths to happiness these days. *The Happiness Toolbox* really delivers. Dr. Paquette makes the compelling case that true happiness is a practiced state of mind you can choose to cultivate through ten well-researched practices that deepen your happiness from the inside out. The dozens of step-by-step What-Why-How exercises are not only easy, even delightful, to do, they are effective. The benefits to your deepening happiness will last a lifetime. "

-**Linda Graham, MFT**
Author of *Bouncing Back: Rewiring Your Brain for Maximum Resilience and Well-Being*

"*The Happiness Toolbox* provides simple, easy-to-use skills grounded in scientific research to help you become happier and healthier. With practical tips and useful exercises, this book is a must-read for anyone looking to boost their well-being and life satisfaction."

-**Nataly Kogan**, author of *Happier Now: How to Stop Chasing Perfection and Embrace Everyday Moments (Even the Difficult Ones)*

"A must-read for everyone who wants to improve their quality of life and well-being. *The Happiness Toolbox* provides a comprehensive guide to creating the life you want. Full of practical tools and exercises to help you maintain lasting behavioral change."

-**Avigail Lev, PsyD**, director of the Bay Area CBT Center, and coauthor of *Acceptance and Commitment Therapy for Interpersonal Problems, The Interpersonal Problems Workbook, and Acceptance and Commitment Therapy for Couples*

"Once again Dr. Paquette has done an excellent job distilling the main factors that increase happiness—life satisfaction. Building on his previous book, he has laid out practical exercises that are both fun and informative in a workbook format. He makes sense of the sometimes confusing literature and hype about happiness, bringing it down to earth to enrich your life. I recommend it highly!"

-**John B. Arden, PhD, ABPP**, author of
Mind-Brain-Gene and *Brain2Brain*

"*The Happiness Toolbox* provides a fresh perspective toward creating positive mindsets among children and adults. The workbook presents a variety of engaging and informative activities to build and strengthen components of psychological well-being and resiliency. Incorporating topics like gratitude, kindness, and compassion within clinical practice is rewarding to both the client and clinician. This is a must have tool for any mental health provider."

-**Lisa Weed Phifer, D.Ed., NCSP**, co-author of
CBT Toolbox for Children and Adolescents

About the Author

. . . .

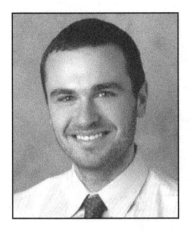

Jonah Paquette, Psy.D., is a licensed clinical psychologist, speaker, and author. He is the Director of Clinical Training at Kaiser Permanente Vallejo in the San Francisco Bay Area, where he runs an APA-accredited postdoctoral residency program and oversees a team of over 30 mental health trainees. In addition to this role, he conducts group and individual psychotherapy, performs crisis evaluations, and teaches a weekly class on happiness for the clinic. Beyond his clinical work and writing, Dr. Paquette offers training and consultation to therapists and organizations on the promotion of happiness, and conducts professional workshops around the country. A frequent media contributor, he has been featured in print, online, television, and radio outlets as well. In addition to this book, Dr. Paquette is the author of *Real Happiness: Proven Paths for Contentment, Peace, and Well-Being* (PESI Publishing, 2015), a research-based self-help book in which he distills the key findings in the field of happiness research, and offers user-friendly tools to achieve lasting well-being.

Table of Contents

. . . .

Preface

· · · · · · · · ·

About 75 years ago, a group of nuns entering convents in the Midwest were asked to complete a simple, seemingly insignificant task. They were invited to write a very brief autobiographical statement describing their lives and exploring their feelings about joining their religious order. The statements were often quite concise, only a few short sentences in length, and perhaps some of the nuns never thought of this experience again from that point on. They certainly could never have imagined that their words would serve as one of the most significant resources ever discovered in the field of happiness research. As an example, one of the letters read as follows:

> I was born in 1909, the eldest of seven children. My candidate year was spent in the motherhouse, teaching chemistry. With God's grace, I intend to do my best for our order, for the spread of religion, and for my personal sanctification.

Take a moment and reflect on these words. What stands out to you? How might you describe the language used by this particular nun? Contrast the above statement with another letter written by a different nun, which read:

> God started my life off well by bestowing upon me a grace of inestimable value. The past year, which I have spent as a candidate studying at Notre Dame College has been a very happy one. Now I look forward with eager joy to receiving the Holy Habit of Our Lady and to a life of union with Love Divine.

Compared to the first, we can see that this second letter is filled with expressions of joy, happiness, and positive affect. We might even be able to conjure an image of what these two nuns might be like in person, and get a sense of their personalities just from this brief statement. But why does this even matter? And can these words shed any light on anything more meaningful about these nuns?

Deborah Danner and David Snowden, two psychologists and happiness researchers, happened to be intrigued by the differences found in these letters and decided to investigate the link between writing style and subsequent longevity and health outcomes. In order to do this, they sorted through 180 of these letters and coded them according to their overall level of *language positivity*. For example, autobiographical statements that included many words such as "grateful," "joy," "happy," or "love" were deemed to have high language positivity, while those that didn't were rated as less positive. Danner and Snowden then divided the letters into quartiles, ranging from the happiest 25% to the least cheerful 25%. After doing so, they attempted to find out whether there was a connection between expressed happiness in the nuns' letters and their longevity. As it turned out, the findings were nothing short of remarkable.

In analyzing the data, Snowden and Danner found that the nuns in the top quartile lived an average of 10 years longer than those in the lowest quartile. Moreover, over half of the most cheerful nuns were still alive at the age of 93, compared to only 18% of the least cheerful. Best of all, it should be noted that nuns happen to make excellent research subjects. Indeed, we know that they were living in the same towns, had access to the same medical care, breathed the same air, and lived very similar lifestyles from one another. If not these factors, what then accounted for the vast differences in longevity and health? Their level of happiness, expressed even in that brief moment in time, appears to hold the answers to this riddle. And that is where our journey to greater happiness will begin.

At the core, all of us want to be happy. If you were to ask the average person on the street what they want most in life, there would be a high likelihood that their response would be "to be happy." Psychologist Ed Diener, one of the world's foremost experts on happiness research, has pointed out that throughout the world and across many cultures, personal happiness (and the happiness of those we love most) ranks right at the top of what people want most in life. And indeed, most of our major life decisions, including marriage, having children, changing jobs, or moving to a new city, are made with happiness in mind as our desired goal. But what does this word "happiness" even mean? Is it something that we can create or is it something we are born with? And is it something that we can actually change in a lasting way?

These questions, and more, will be explored in the pages to come. In the opening chapter of this workbook, we'll explore the nature of happiness and the benefits of being happy, as well as discuss some of the key barriers and roadblocks that get in the way of our well-being. The bulk of this book will focus on a series of key principles for lasting well-being, complete with more than 60 practical, science-based exercises that can boost happiness starting today.

Can we become lastingly happier, and achieve greater purpose and joy in life? Absolutely. It will take effort and commitment, like learning any new skill, but the rewards are great. Beyond simply feeling happier, it is likely that you can achieve a host of other gains that have been associated with greater happiness, including but not limited to:

- Stronger relationships
- Better job/school performance
- Improved physical health
- Longer lifespan
- Fewer illnesses

Best of all, the latest research suggests that happiness is best thought of as a *practiced state of mind*. Although there are genetic and environmental factors (which we'll get to), much of our happiness is determined by our mindset, our habits, and the practices we engage in. Over the past 15 years there's been an explosion in the research on how we can become happier. Rather than being something we stumble upon, research has identified a handful of practices that can foster lasting happiness and well-being. These include:

- Gratitude
- Kindness and compassion
- Self-compassion
- Mindfulness
- Optimism
- Interpersonal connection
- Letting go of resentment
- Identifying and using your strengths
- Savoring the good
- Caring for your body and health

Although these principles might seem daunting or far-fetched in some way, one of the most encouraging findings to emerge from the research on happiness is that they are easy to achieve. This book will show you how to take these findings, make sense of them, and apply them to your own life.

My motivation for writing this book is to share these keys to well-being to help you to become lastingly happier. Some of you may be familiar with my last book, *Real Happiness: Proven Paths for Contentment, Peace, and Well-Being*, which provides an overview of many of the latest findings in the field of happiness and well-being. This book will focus a bit less on the background and research side of things, and more on the "how-to" part of the happiness equation. In the pages to come, you'll find over 60 empirically-validated practices designed to boost your mental and emotional well-being. Best of all, they are designed to be realistic and practical, and can be implemented into your life starting today. From the bottom of my heart, thank you for taking the time to check out my book, and for taking this important step towards enhancing your own well-being.

Defining Happiness

. . . .

> *Happiness is a choice*
> *that requires effort at times.*
> —Aeschylus

> *Happiness depends*
> *upon ourselves.*
> —Aristotle

When I was growing up, I was an avid collector of baseball cards. I would collect cards of all my favorite players (especially if they played for the New York Yankees), study them for hours on end, and memorize the statistics that were contained on the back of the cards. Some of you reading this book may have done the same. I spent the bulk of my "studies" gazing upon the back of the card, trying to decipher which players the Yankees should pursue, and determining which players might be poised for a break-out season and future superstardom. As you might imagine, I did not go on many dates when I was a young man!

While I spent hours reviewing statistics such as batting averages, home runs, and runs scored, I didn't spend very much time gazing at the front of the cards, which contained the actual photograph of the ballplayer. Little did I realize at the time, but I was holding in my hands information not only about who the best players were, but also valuable clues on happiness and health.

. . .

Reflect for a moment about the last time you posed for a picture. Perhaps it was at a recent family gathering, at a work function, or during a night out on the town with friends. Do you remember how you smiled? As we know from personal experience, there are many ways to smile in front of the camera when the person snapping the picture says "cheese." There's the somewhat strained, uncomfortable, forced smile we might generate when our mind is elsewhere or if we're standing next to someone we don't particularly care for. And then there's that big, robust, genuine smile we feel when we're experiencing true happiness or joy.

Although these differences may not seem like a big deal, they have some pretty big implications. Scientists have in fact distinguished these two types of smiles, and have dubbed them as "Duchenne" versus "non-Duchenne" smiles. The name refers to a French physician named Guillaume Duchenne, who many years ago was the first to identify the differences between these types of smiles. A "non-Duchenne" smile is the somewhat forced, unexcited smile and involves only the muscles around our mouth. A "Duchenne" smile, on the other hand, involves both the muscles around our mouth as well as those surrounding our eyes, with the result being a full-faced expression of happiness often complete with "crow's feet" around our eyes.

Returning to my beloved baseball card collection, you may have noticed that ballplayers (like the rest of us) strike many different sorts of poses when having their picture taken. Some give a very robust, full-faced "Duchenne" smile, while others give a more forced grin. Still others give no smile at all, or may even give something of a scowl to the camera. But what's in a smile, anyway? And can a smile, or lack of one, actually point to something more significant or meaningful about a person, their happiness, or their lives in general?

As it happens, a pair of researchers sought to answer these very questions. Psychology professors Ernest Abel and Michael Kruger of Wayne State University aimed to determine whether there was any connection between a ballplayer's smile and his longevity. To do so, they examined the photographs of Major League Baseball players from the 1952 season, and sorted them according to their smiles (ranging from full, "Duchenne" smiles on the one hand, to those exhibiting no smile at all).

Remarkably, they discovered a huge connection between the intensity of a player's smile and his subsequent lifespan. Specifically, players who displayed no smile in their photographs lived an average lifespan of 72 years, while those exhibiting a slight smile lived until the age of 75 on average. Amazingly, the ballplayers who displayed a full "Duchenne" smile lived even longer, to an average age of 80!

And it turns out that there's nothing particularly special about baseball players when it comes to this. Indeed, another renowned study in the field of happiness research looked at the yearbook photos of college graduates, and examined the link between one's smile in these photos and later outcomes such as marriage, relationship satisfaction, career achievement, and life satisfaction. When researchers examined this link, they discovered that those individuals with the fullest "Duchenne" smiles were more likely to be married, and their marriages were more likely to be rated as satisfying. They scored higher in overall life satisfaction measures, and were more able to manage stress. They even achieved greater success at the workplace.

While these studies are not in themselves definitive, they nonetheless speak to something important. Namely, they underscore the importance of being happy. Although a photograph represents but a thin slice of time in a person's life, it seems to point out some valuable clues when it comes to a person's happiness, longevity, and health. We often (appropriately) consider happiness to be a worthy goal in and of itself, but some of the most exciting research to burst onto the scene since the early 2000's has been the discovery of the powerful connection between happiness and a number of desirable outcomes. In this chapter we'll explore some of the many benefits that have been linked to increased happiness, life satisfaction, and psychological well-being. But before doing so, let's back up a step and explore a simple yet crucial question: What does it even mean to be happy?

Defining Happiness

What does the word "happiness" mean to you? What emotions does it evoke, and what images spring to mind when you reflect on it? In your experience, what would you say are the key ingredients of true, meaningful happiness? Take a moment, close your eyes if you'd like, and consider what this concept means for you.

How would you define happiness?

_____

_____

_____

_____

One of the many challenges of happiness research is the fact that the very notion of happiness can be quite difficult to define. Indeed, happiness is a topic that garners a great deal of attention; yet pinning down exactly what it is can prove elusive. There have been many different opinions over the years on what comprises true happiness. Mahatma Gandhi, for example, considered happiness to be something that occurred **"when what you think, what you say, and what you do are in harmony."** In contrast, the French physician and philosopher Albert Schweitzer once jokingly declared that happiness is "nothing more than good health and a bad memory." Though these definitions may be interesting, they do little in terms of helping us understand happiness from a scientific perspective.

An important contribution of the positive psychology movement in recent years has been helping us gain a common understanding of this unwieldy concept of happiness. For example, one of the world's foremost happiness experts, Martin Seligman, initially defined happiness as being comprised of three separate yet interconnected elements:

- Positive emotions
- Engagement
- Meaning

For Seligman, "positive emotions" refers to experiencing pleasant emotions regarding our past, present, and future, and is marked by the experience of generally positive mood-states across these domains. "Engagement" denotes the idea of flow, a state of mind in which we are so engrossed in the task at hand that time seemingly stops. Finally, "meaning" refers to the idea of being connected to a cause greater than oneself. According to this viewpoint of happiness, true well-being consists of a combination of each of these three components, with a sense of meaning or purpose serving as the most important ingredient.

Seligman has since expanded this definition of happiness to include two additional components to the three outlined above: *Relationships* and *Accomplishments*. Reflecting these, Seligman's updated conceptualization of well-being can be remembered by the acronym PERMA, which denotes the following five elements:

- *P*ositive Emotions
- *R*elationships
- *A*ccomplishments
- *E*ngagement
- *M*eaning

Another prominent researcher in the field of positive psychology, Sonja Lyubomirsky, has described happiness as "the experience of joy, contentment, or positive well-being, combined with a sense that one's life is good, meaningful, or worthwhile." As with Seligman's definition of happiness, this one too emphasizes the multiple layers of true happiness and well-being. Rather than consisting merely of pleasant, fleeting emotions, real happiness also includes a deeper sense of meaning, satisfaction with one's life, and purpose.

Throughout this book, in order to help us remain on the same page and have a common understanding of happiness, we will consider well-being and happiness to similarly consist of:

- A strong presence of *pleasant and positive emotional states*, both in the present moment as well as towards the past and future;
- A *sense of connection* to those around us, as well as to our pursuits, vocations, and activities;
- A deep, underlying feeling of *life satisfaction*; and
- A sense of *meaning and purpose* that can anchor us even when fleeting positive emotions may not be present.

As you can see, the sort of happiness that's being described above is a much deeper and richer phenomenon than what we might expect. Whereas the "Hollywood" depiction of happiness focuses primarily on intense positive emotions such as joy, ebullience, or pleasure, happiness as considered by positive psychologists is a bit of a different experience. Positive emotions are certainly a part of the picture, but equally (perhaps even more so) important are those deeper experiences of meaning and purpose, satisfaction with our lives, and connection to both people and causes in our lives.

What do you make of these definitions of happiness? Does anything surprise you? In what way do they fit (or not) with how you tend to think of happiness? Take a moment and reflect on what comes to mind:

_____

_____

_____

_____

Happiness: A Timeless Pursuit

Although much of the research on happiness is recent—having emerged since the early 2000's since the birth of positive psychology—it should be pointed out that interest in happiness dates back centuries. Indeed, the topic of well-being has been a concern of philosophers, theologians, and scholars for thousands of years. From Greek and Roman philosophers in the West, to Buddhist and Confucian thinkers in the East, questions related to the "good life" have certainly been prominent throughout the years.

Within the field of psychology, the lion's share of the focus has historically been centered on the reduction of misery and the management of illness. Nonetheless, there have been a handful of pioneers over the years who have attempted to investigate issues such as contentment, thriving, happiness, and flourishing. These individuals include luminaries such as Abraham Maslow, Carl Rogers, and Marie Jahoda, among others. For them, questions related to fulfillment, happiness, and optimal functioning were considered critical to understanding the human condition.

Despite a longstanding interest in the topic, the emergence of positive psychology has proven to be a remarkable turning point in the field of happiness research, and has led to a tremendous boom within both the mainstream and academia. For the first time in history, researchers have begun to approach our timeless interest in happiness by utilizing rigorous methods of scientific inquiry.

Today, we know more about how to boost happiness and well-being than at any other point in history. Best of all, rather than having to rely on testimonials or theory, we can rely on science and research to guide us in our search for greater well-being. Recent research has helped us to understand which strategies do and do not boost our well-being in the long term. Above all, the aim of this book is to present these findings to you, and to teach you the necessary skills for a happier life.

The Benefits of Being Happy

If you were to take a moment and reflect on what changes you could make to improve your life, increase your lifespan, or strengthen your health, what comes to mind? Take a moment and jot down a few quick thoughts:

1. _____

2. _____

3. _____

4. _____

If you're like most people, perhaps you considered starting a new exercise regimen, changing your diet, or reducing your substance use. Each of these would undoubtedly be a great place to start, and there's research to support each of these ideas when it comes to our health.

But it just so happens that there's another way to improve our health, increase our life expectancy, strengthen our relationships, and even improve our job performance: Namely, becoming a happier person. By doing so, we have the opportunity to vastly improve our mental and emotional well-being, strengthen our physical health, and transform our lives. Best of all, the latest research suggests that it's not a case in which people become happier because of these benefits; rather, the reverse appears to be true—people who are happier tend to be healthier and more fulfilled in life.

We all know from personal experience that being happy is a good thing in and of itself. Indeed, for most of us, personal happiness (or the happiness of those we love most) factors heavily into many of our major life decisions. But though it undoubtedly feels good on an emotional level to be happy, it turns out that this is just the tip of the iceberg. In fact, as more research comes out related to happiness and well-being, the more we understand just how critical it is across a large number of areas in our life.

What sorts of benefits might you expect as a result of greater happiness? What impact might increased well-being have in different areas of your life?

_____

_____

_____

One of the most exciting findings to emerge from the happiness literature is that happiness doesn't just feel good—it's good for us as well. Although happier people perform better than less happy individuals across a number of domains, four areas in particular stand out: improved psychological health, better physical health, stronger social relationships, and enhanced cognitive performance.

Better Psychological Health

Negative emotional states, such as anger, sadness, or fear, prompt very narrow, survival-oriented behaviors. As an example, think of the "fight or flight" response that we experience when we feel acutely anxious or fearful. Our focus narrows, we perceive threats more intensely, and our mind and body go on high alert. This deeply ingrained tendency is wonderful when it comes to things like survival and spreading our gene pool. Unfortunately, it's pretty lousy when it comes to our own happiness.

Whereas negative emotions prompt the type of responses outlined above, positive and pleasant emotions have the opposite function in our lives. As psychologist Barbara Fredrickson has shown, positive emotional states serve to "broaden and build" our personal resources. We seek out novel experiences, connect with others interpersonally, and think more creatively. Psychologically, positive emotional states help buffer against negative experiences, increase our resilience, and can actually help to "undo" the effects of negative emotions on both a psychological and even physiological level. Moreover, this cycle has a way of feeding on itself, such that Fredrickson has dubbed it the "upward spiral" of well-being.

In recent years, there has been a groundswell of research emerging on the psychological benefits of becoming a happier person. By fostering the skills you'll be working on in the pages to come (such as gratitude, compassion, and interpersonal connection), studies show that doing so can buffer against a wide range of psychological problems including depression, anxiety, stress, and more. These skills can be utilized not only to treat these sorts of problems, but to buffer against their recurrence as well. Overall, from a psychological standpoint, it certainly pays to become a happier person. But although this is a worthy goal in and of itself, some of the most impressive benefits to boosting one's happiness lie in other parts of our lives.

Better Physical Health

Reflect for a moment on the last time you visited your doctor for a health check-up. You probably remember being asked a number of questions about your health habits, such as how often you exercise, what your diet consists of, how much alcohol you consume, and so forth. This makes good sense, because these sorts of behavioral choices can have a tremendous impact on your physical health. But do you know what else makes a huge difference when it comes to your health? You guessed it—becoming a happier person!

There have been a large number of studies to suggest that happiness and well-being not only feel good—they're good for us as well. Research suggests that happier individuals live longer lives, have stronger immune system functioning, and get sick less frequently than less happy people. In one longitudinal study, it was found that happier people were less likely to fall prey to chronic health conditions like high blood pressure and diabetes, and were even less likely to struggle with substance use problems. By actively cultivating our own happiness and attending to it with the importance it deserves, it appears that we can become healthier too.

More Fulfilling Social Relationships

Renowned psychiatrist George Vaillant once famously stated, "happiness is love—full stop." The sort of "love" Vaillant was describing was essentially close interpersonal connection, and the impact that it has on a person's psychological well-being. In recent years, numerous studies have supported this notion—that our own happiness is inextricably connected to our interpersonal relationships. Moreover, there appears to be a bidirectional relationship between these two variables. In other words, happier people tend to have stronger, more meaningful relationships with those around them; but by also consciously fostering these relationships, we can have a powerful effect on our own happiness.

Better Cognitive Performance

You may be wondering about whether happiness might have a negative effect on things like job performance and achievement. Indeed, we sometimes run into the stereotype of happy people lacking the "edge" they need to succeed in these realms. But do "happy people finish last," to borrow an old phrase? Actually, research suggests that the exact opposite is true: **Happier people perform better across a range of cognitive tasks, and tend to be more flexible in their thinking as well as being more creative.** These benefits are reflected in studies of both students and adults in the workplace, with findings suggesting that happier individuals perform significantly better than their less happy counterparts. Indeed, happier individuals are more likely to obtain jobs, succeed in those jobs, gain promotions, and earn more money. So it pays to be happy, not just figuratively, but literally as well!

Do the findings outlined above surprise you? What do you think accounts for the powerful connection between happiness and the wide-ranging parts of our lives outlined above? Write your thoughts in the space below:

_____

_____

_____

_____

Roadblocks to Well-Being

Have you ever daydreamed about owning a bigger home, purchasing a shiny new car, or getting a long-awaited promotion at work? If so, you've probably done this for a very specific reason: You believed it would make you a happier person. We all fall into this pattern of thinking and acting, and many of our major life choices are made with the goal of happiness in mind. Indeed, everything from our relationship choices to where we decide to live is influenced by an internal (often unconscious) decision about whether it will make us happier.

Take a moment and think about what sorts of things you've expected to bring you happiness over the years. Common examples might include finding a new job, entering a new exciting relationship, moving to a new city, and so forth. Use the space below to write down some examples that come to mind:

_____

_____

_____

_____

The idea that if something good happens to us, then we'll be happy, is a very common belief that most of us fall prey to from time to time. I call it the "if/then" style of happiness seeking, and it tends to promote the idea that **if** we achieve some desirable outcome in our lives, **then** we'll be happy. For example, we might tell ourselves that **if** we were to purchase a beautiful new home, or **if** we were to move to a new city, **then** we would be happy.

Although the "if/then" style of thinking is certainly seductive when it comes to our happiness, we all know from personal experience that these sorts of external changes rarely lead to lasting and true well-being. It's not that good things happening to us don't make us happy, because they do. It's just that positive changes like those outlined above make us less happy than we expect, and the gains that we achieve last a much shorter time than we expect.

A classic example of this phenomenon can be seen in studies conducted on lottery winners. Just as we might expect, winning the lottery typically leads to an immediate and sizable boost in terms of a person's happiness. The problem is that these gains are quite fleeting, almost akin to a happiness "sugar high." Indeed, within a handful of months, most lottery winners return to their original baseline level of happiness and life-satisfaction.

As it turns out there are many examples like this, of positive changes in our lives that we expect to lead to lasting increases in happiness but don't. Some common examples of things that many people expect to make them happier but don't in the long run include (but are not limited to):

- **Money and Income:** Once basic needs are met, additional money makes very little, if any, difference in terms of a person's happiness level. Some estimates suggest that once an annual income of roughly $75,000 is met, additional money makes no difference when it comes to making a person happier.
- **Geography:** Studies show that with the exception of people suffering from Seasonal Affective Disorder, the average person's happiness is not affected by where they live geographically. Differences do exist when comparing countries, but that is more related to systems of government and/or oppression. Climate and geography, however, do not appear to play a role in happiness.
- **Getting Married:** Research suggests that following an initial boost in happiness (roughly 18 months on average), married individuals tend to revert back to their previous happiness baseline levels.
- **Having Children:** Although there is conflicting research on this topic, numerous studies suggest that day-to-day levels of happiness and life satisfaction fall among parents following the birth of a child, and are particularly low during the teenage years. Only once a child moves off to college or leaves the home do happiness scores tend to revert back to their original baseline among parents.
- **Physical Attractiveness:** Studies show that the people who score the lowest of any profession for happiness are models.

What do you make of the previous findings? Do any surprise you? Write down your reactions below:

_____

_____

_____

_____

But why do all these seemingly wonderful things have such little (if any) benefit to our long-term happiness? The answer lies in a few key areas, which we will now briefly turn our attention to. As it turns out, there are a handful of factors that make it hard for us to feel lastingly happy, three of which we will briefly discuss below.

Key Barriers to Happiness

Hedonic Adaptation

Human beings have a remarkable ability to adapt to changes in their environment. For example, think of the last time you entered a dark movie theater—at first it was probably quite difficult to see, but shortly thereafter your eyes adjusted and you could make your way to your seat. Or consider the way that a rather unpleasant odor stops being so noticeable after a short while. These examples demonstrate a process called *physiological adaptation*—in other words, our ability to adapt to physiological changes in our environment.

A similar process occurs when it comes to our happiness, and is known as hedonic adaptation. This refers to the idea that we tend to "adjust" to so-called hedonic (pleasant) changes in our environment, and find ourselves back to our baseline level of happiness rather quickly. It helps explain, for example, why lottery winners revert to their previous levels of happiness only a few months after they win an enormous sum of money. But it also helps explain why, for example, accident victims who lose the use of their legs return to their prior level of happiness in a somewhat similar time frame.

A key take-home message is that hedonic adaptation is neither good nor bad. In fact, the same process that drags us down after something wonderful happens helps bring us back up following tragedy. So just as financial windfalls and strokes of good fortune fade over time, so too do the painful emotions associated with loss and setbacks. But due to its tendency to "undo" the benefits of positive changes in our lives, hedonic adaptation serves as a powerful barrier to lastingly increasing our happiness. And it helps explain why so many of the factors that we normally think will make us lastingly happier (such as more money, a change in appearance, entering a new relationship, and so forth) lose their luster after a short while.

The Genetic Lottery

Our genes play a powerful role in many areas of our lives, from our personalities and our appearance, to our risk of certain illnesses and diseases. As it turns out, our genes also play a powerful role when it comes to our happiness levels. Through researching both fraternal and identical twins, as well as non-twin siblings, scientists have come to find that a large portion of our happiness is genetically influenced.

How much of an influence do genes have in this area? Estimates vary, but most studies seem to suggest that our genes account for as much as 40-50% of our level of happiness. If you've ever known someone, for example, who seems to take setbacks in stride, or always seems to see the glass as "half full," there's a strong likelihood that that individual may have hit the genetic lottery when it comes to happiness. Conversely, we all know people for whom being happy seems to be an uphill struggle, and those individuals may have been less fortunate when it comes to a "genetic" predisposition to happiness.

Although our genes play an important role in determining our happiness baseline or "set point," it's crucial that we don't take this message too far. Indeed, it's better to think of it being akin to weight: Some of us may be naturally heavy or thin, and in the absence of proper diet or exercise we may drift towards where our genes predispose us. However, this does *not* mean that we're doomed to be mere reflections of our genetic "set point," and we are all able to transform ourselves based on the choices and behaviors we engage in, whether in terms of weight or happiness.

Our "Negative" Brain

Have you ever felt as if a dozen good things can happen to you in a day, but a single bad experience is all you can think about when you get home that night? You're not alone, and in fact we can thank another key barrier to happiness for this sort of experience: our very own brain. When it comes to our happiness, it's worth remembering that our brains developed over the millennia not to be happy, but rather to survive. And sometimes the very things that helped us to survive as a species also make it hard to feel lastingly content, peaceful, and happy.

Life was quite difficult for our early ancestors, with constant threats of famine, warfare, and natural disaster surrounding them at all times. In order to help us to survive, we became highly attuned to threats and danger, and to focusing on the negative aspects of our environment rather than the positive ones. And although our world has changed in many ways since that time period, it's a drop in the bucket from an evolutionary standpoint. As a result, we are still operating with much of the same basic "machinery" that our ancestors did hundreds of thousands of years ago.

Our brain has a built-in "negativity bias" in order to help us survive. This means we remember bad outcomes much more easily than good ones, and negative events impact us much more strongly than positive ones. This negativity bias has been shown to be so strong, that some studies suggest we need to experience several positive events during our day to overcome just a single negative one. The neuropsychologist Rick Hanson has described our brain thusly as being like "Teflon for good, and Velcro for bad." This negativity bias leads us to feel unhappy and stressed much of the time, especially if we are not actively working on shifting out mindset towards the positive.

Think back on a time where you fell prey to one of these "happiness barriers." Perhaps it was "hedonic adaptation" causing you to lose joy from something that once gave you a great deal of pleasure, or your "negativity bias" causing you to lose sight of the good aspects of your life. Take a moment and write about it in the space below:

_____

_____

_____

_____

What's really under our control?

Although the barriers to happiness listed previously are formidable, they are *not* insurmountable. And despite all the factors that make it difficult to become happier (such as hedonic adaptation, our genes, and the negativity bias), it is absolutely possible to become lastingly happier. We just need to look in the right place, and foster the right kinds of habits.

If the bad news (for some) is that genes account for up to 40-50% of a person's happiness level, the good news (for all of us) is that our circumstances around us account for only a small portion of our happiness—as little as 10%. Keep in mind, these sorts of external circumstances (how much money we earn, whether we are married or not, where we live, etc.) are where we tend to look to become happier. Yet these things (which can be very difficult to change in the first place), account for only a small portion of our happiness level.

The best news of all is that we are left with an entire 40-50% entirely in our control, and determined by the choices we make, the mindset we cultivate, and the habits we engage in. That portion of our lives is what this book will focus on. The coming chapters will review 10 core principles that have been shown to create lasting increases in our happiness levels. Each has been researched extensively, backed by numerous scientific studies, and each has been linked to meaningful changes in a person's happiness over time and with practice. Best of all, none of these principles are fixed; rather, they are all learnable, and changeable, with effort.

How to Use This Book

In the pages to come, we'll be reviewing 10 core principles for lasting happiness. They include:

- Gratitude
- Kindness and compassion
- Self-compassion
- Mindfulness
- Optimism
- Interpersonal connection
- Forgiveness
- Cultivating strengths
- Savoring the good
- Cultivating health and wellness

Each chapter will focus on one of these core principles, and will begin with a brief overview of the key benefits associated with each, including the impact on our health, our psychological well-being, and even our brain. Following the brief overview, each chapter will then include a handful (usually five to seven) of practices designed to help integrate the approach into your life.

Each of the practices contained in this book are organized in a similar way. At the top of each exercise below the title, you'll find a brief listing of the practice's duration, frequency, and difficulty level. See the example below:

Duration: Lists how long the practice takes, which usually ranges from 5-30 minutes.

Frequency: Provides guidance on how often to do it. Some exercises can be done just once, while others are done on a daily basis.

Level of Difficulty: Ranges from Easy to Moderate to Difficult.

You will then be provided with a brief **overview** of the practice, followed by **instructions** to guide you in how to put the practice into use. The overview provides a brief bit of information and rationale for the practice, while the instructions give you precise guidance on how to go about using the practice in your everyday life.

Following the instructions, you'll find a section titled **How and Why it Works,** which provides a bit more information on how each particular exercise can make such a positive impact on your happiness and well-being. Below this section you'll see another section entitled **Notes/Impressions** along with space for your own writing. This is meant to give you an opportunity to jot down any experiences and feelings that come up in doing each practice that you'd like to remember for later, including what worked and what didn't, or anything in particular you'd like to remember about the practice for later.

As you work your way through the book, feel free to adapt the exercises and be flexible based on what works for you and your preferences. The biggest key is that you don't simply read the exercise, but regularly practice it and integrate it into your life. When we do that, we can harness the portion of happiness that is under our control, and become a lastingly happier person. I wish you good luck in your journey to happiness.

CHAPTER ONE

The Pursuit of Happiness

> *What is the meaning of life?*
> *To be happy and useful.*
>
> —His Holiness, the Dalai Lama

What Is Happiness?

There have been many definitions of happiness over the years, but positive psychologists have centered on a handful of core components and themes when it comes to defining happiness and well-being. These include:

- **Positive emotions** about the past, present, and future;
- A sense of **connection** to those around us, as well as our pursuits, vocations, and activities;
- A deep, underlying feeling of **life satisfaction;** and
- A sense of **meaning and purpose**, and that our lives are worthwhile.

Better still, happiness is best thought of as a *skill*, or a *practiced state of mind*. This means that through practice and effort, we can all become happier over time.

How Much Can We Control?

According to research, our happiness level is determined by a combination of our genes, our environment, and our own actions. While genes account for roughly half of our happiness level, our life circumstances account for only around 10% of our overall well-being. This means that upwards of 40% (or more) is under our control through our thoughts and our actions.

What Gets in the Way of Happiness?

The following factors can get in the way of our happiness:

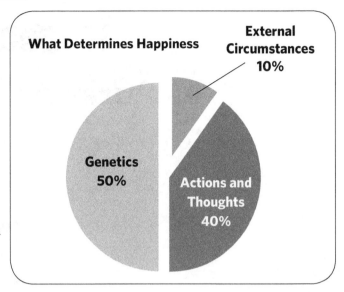

- **Hedonic adaptation:** We tend to adjust to changes in our lives, both good and bad. This helps explain why even wonderful changes in our lives (like winning the lottery!) have only a temporary impact on our happiness level. Hedonic adaptation helps explain why we can often feel as if we're "running in place" when it comes to our happiness, and can struggle to achieve lasting gains.
- **The "impact bias":** We overestimate the impact of very large changes in our lives (such as a new job, a new relationship, or moving to a new city), when smaller, day-to-day things can make a bigger difference.
- **A "negative" brain:** Our brains were built for survival, not to be happy. That's why negative or painful experiences stick with us much more than good ones, and why setbacks can feel so difficult to shake off. Luckily, the notion of neuroplasticity suggests that over time, our habits and behaviors can actually change our brain on a structural level, and can help us to overcome this "negativity bias."
- **Our genes:** As much as half of our happiness appears to come from our genes, according to a number of studies looking at happiness levels in twins (compared to siblings in general). While this may seem like a lot, it still gives us plenty of room to work with and makes a big difference to our level of happiness.

What Are the Benefits of Being Happy?

Happiness comes with a wealth of benefits. Some of them include:

- **Better health:** Happier people have stronger immune systems, suffer from fewer chronic diseases, and even have longer lifespans according to numerous studies.
- **Psychological benefits:** Happier individuals struggle with fewer mental health difficulties such as depression or anxiety, and are more resilient in the face of adversity and setbacks.
- **Interpersonal benefits:** Individuals who are happier tend to have more friendships and stronger social networks. They are more likely to get married and stay married, and are even rated by their partners in more positive terms.
- **Better overall functioning:** Rather than being an outcome or by product of success, recent research suggests that happiness is actually a cause for success! Happier people perform better at both school and at work, are more likely to get hired for jobs, are more likely to be promoted, and even earn more money.

What Are the Keys to Lasting Happiness?

These practices have been strongly linked to lasting well-being:

- **Gratitude:** Studies show that fostering a sense of gratitude and appreciation for the positive aspects of our lives has a powerful impact on our own happiness level. By shifting our focus towards the good in our lives, research suggests we can become much happier.
- **Kindness and compassion:** Another crucial element of well-being comes through expressions of kindness and caring towards others. Indeed, numerous studies show that giving to others, whether through formal volunteer work or other means, is one of the most powerful ways to boost our own happiness.
- **Self-Compassion:** Around 80% of people tend to be harder on themselves than they are on others. Unfortunately, this sort of self-criticism takes a tremendous toll on our well-being. Self-Compassion—learning to treat ourselves with kindness and caring—has been shown to have powerful benefits on our mental and physical health.
- **Mindfulness:** Some studies suggest that we spend roughly half of our waking hours mentally detached from the present moment; in other words, we may be physically in one place, but mentally we are somewhere else. This same research suggests that the more our mind wanders, the less happy we tend to be. Mindfulness—the ability to be nonjudgmentally aware in the present moment—has been shown to have immense benefits to our happiness and well-being, along with our physical health.
- **Optimism:** We've all heard it said that it's best to see the glass as "half full," but recent research underscores the importance of optimism to both our mental and physical well-being. Indeed, optimists tend to be both happier and healthier than pessimists across many different areas.
- **Interpersonal connection:** We live in a world of infinite connection these days thanks to technology and social media. Unfortunately, some studies suggest that the quality of our interpersonal connections has deteriorated as the quantity has gone up. This is unfortunate, because much research shows that one of the best ways to reliably increase our level of happiness is to enhance the quality of our closest interpersonal relationships.
- **Forgiveness:** When we are hurt, anger is a natural response. But holding onto anger for months, or even years, can have a toxic effect on our mental and physical health. Learning to let go of this anger can free us, and the practice of forgiveness has been linked to a number of powerful benefits to our health and happiness.
- **Using our strengths:** Learning to identify and harness our own personal strengths has been shown to have a number of benefits when it comes to boosting our own level of happiness and achieving a greater sense of meaning and purpose in our lives.
- **Savoring positive experiences:** Sometimes good things can happen in our lives but we quickly move onto the next thing. Similarly, because negative experiences have a much more powerful effect on us, it's easy to lose sight of the good experiences that might occur each day. The skill of savoring helps us to amplify and draw out positive and pleasant experiences, to better allow them to "sink in" from a happiness standpoint.
- **Caring for our bodies and health:** During times of stress, it's particularly easy to lose sight of self-care, and our health is one of the first areas to suffer. By attending to our sleep, exercise patterns, and even the food that we eat, we can lay the groundwork for increased happiness and well-being.

CHAPTER TWO

Gratitude

> *He is a wise man who does not grieve for the things which he has not, but rejoices for those which he has.*
>
> —Epictetus

> *When eating bamboo sprouts, remember the man who planted them.*
>
> —Chinese Proverb

What Is Gratitude?

The world's foremost expert on gratitude, Robert Emmons, defines gratitude as "a sense of wonder, thankfulness, and appreciation for life." He notes that gratitude consists of two separate but interconnected steps:

- First, we acknowledge the goodness that is present in our lives.
- Second, we recognize that the source of these blessings lies at least partially outside of our own doing.

Gratitude can be an external, visible behavior, such as the act of thanking someone. But it can also be a more private or internal process, such as acknowledging and reflecting on the good aspects of our lives.

Why Practice Gratitude?

An explosion of research on the many benefits of gratitude has marked the past decade or so. As it turns out, gratitude is not merely an emotion that feels good; it actually holds the key to a number of psychological, physical, and social benefits as well.

The Psychological Benefits of Gratitude

Studies show that individuals who regularly practice gratitude perform better across a number of areas when it comes to mental and emotional health. Indeed, gratitude has been linked to lower rates of depression, along with helping to buffer against future depressive episodes. It has also been shown to decrease rates of depression and stress, while also enhancing positive mental states such as joy, optimism, and tranquility.

The Health Benefits of Gratitude

Not only are grateful individuals happier, but research suggests that they are healthier as well. Studies have found that individuals who regularly practice gratitude have improved overall physical health, stronger immune systems, and reduced rates of stress-related illnesses. Not only that, but research has linked the practice of gratitude to other benefits such as getting better sleep (as much as an extra hour per night), and exercising more (as much as 90 minutes more per week).

The Interpersonal Benefits of Gratitude

Many studies have shown that grateful individuals have stronger interpersonal relationships, including more satisfying romantic relationships. They also are more altruistic, making them more likely to donate to charities and engage in volunteer work, and they are even able to let go of resentments easier and foster forgiveness.

The Grateful Brain

The practice of gratitude is believed to impact our brain in several ways. First, on a structural level, the practice of gratitude has been linked to two areas of the brain in particular: the *hypothalamus* and the *left prefrontal cortex*. Though small in size, the hypothalamus is mighty in function, and it impacts things like our stress level, our sleep, and even our metabolism. The left prefrontal cortex, conversely, has been linked to positive emotional states, including happiness, compassion, love, and joy.

On a chemical level, gratitude has been linked to several neurotransmitter systems, including serotonin and dopamine. Serotonin influences a number of bodily functions and is thought to be strongly connected to our moods. Low levels of serotonin are thought by some researchers to be linked to higher rates of depression, and gratitude may increase our levels of serotonin in our brain. Dopamine, on the other hand, it considered to be a "feel good" neurotransmitter and plays a role in our ability to anticipate rewards and pleasure. Studies suggest that the practice of gratitude may increase levels of dopamine in our brains.

Three Good Things

. . . .

Duration: 10 minutes

Frequency: Daily, for at least two weeks

Level of Difficulty: Easy/Moderate

Overview: Because of our brain's built-in negativity bias, many of us find ourselves constantly stuck on problems, or ruminating about negative events from our day. This helps to contribute to a host of problems, including depression and anxiety. Research suggests that to combat this tendency of the mind, we must deliberately and consciously shift our attention away from the negative and towards the good. In this exercise, you'll be taking the time to notice and appreciate the positive experiences that occur throughout your day. Over time, this will help shift your focus more naturally to these events.

Instructions: Each night for the next two weeks before you go to bed, write down three things that went well for you that day. These good things can be relatively small, even seemingly minor occurrences throughout your day. Or they can be larger, more significant events. There's no right or wrong answer. Simply write three positive experiences from the day, followed by a brief explanation of your contribution to it, or why you think it happened. To challenge yourself further, and make the exercise even more powerful, I recommend never repeating an item from your list over the course of the two weeks (or longer, if you so choose!).

Example:

Good Thing #1: I had a fulfilling day at work and my sessions with patients went well.

Why this happened/My contribution: I made sure I got plenty of sleep last night, and I tried to be very present and attuned in my sessions.

Good Thing #2: My partner cooked my favorite dinner, spaghetti and meatballs.

Why this happened/My contribution: I expressed gratitude and thanked her the last time she cooked.

Good Thing #3: It was a beautiful and sunny day when I was driving to work.

Why this happened/My contribution: I took the time to notice and appreciate the weather, rather than being stuck on "autopilot" as I drove.

Practice:

Good Thing #1:

_____

_____

_____

Why this happened/My contribution:

_____

_____

_____

Good Thing #2:

_____

_____

_____

Why this happened/My contribution:

_____

_____

_____

Good Thing #3:

_____

_____

_____

Why this happened/My contribution:

_____

_____

_____

Key Points to Consider:

✔ Make sure your "good things" are experiences from the same day you're journaling, rather than more general sources of gratitude.

✔ By never repeating an item on your list, you force yourself to stretch your comfort zone and make the exercise even more powerful.

✔ Don't worry about spelling or grammar.

Make sure you write down your good things; although mentally reflecting on positive experiences never hurts, research suggests that taking the time to actually write them down is much more effective.

How and why it works: As you continue to practice this skill, you'll begin noticing a shift in your outlook and the way you view the world. Rather than focusing on sources of stress or negative things that happened throughout your day, you'll find yourself having more and more appreciation for the positives in your life. Over time, you may even begin to find yourself seeking out things to be grateful for throughout the day, in anticipation of writing in your journal. By becoming more able to notice good things as they occur, and to savor them in hindsight, you'll be able to cultivate a deep sense of gratitude and thereby increase your overall happiness and well-being.

Notes/Impressions:

_____

_____

_____

_____

_____

_____

_____

_____

The Gratitude Journal

. . . .

Duration: 15 minutes

Frequency: 1-3 times/week, for at least six weeks

Level of Difficulty: Easy

Overview: Many of us find our minds drifting invariably towards the negative, replaying setbacks that occurred throughout our day and focusing on perceived shortcomings and worries. Due to our brain's negativity bias, we find ourselves stuck in this loop of unconstructive negativity, which can have a tremendous impact on our mental and emotional well-being. Creating a gratitude journal can help bring awareness instead to some of the more overarching, stable sources of gratitude and joy in our lives.

Instructions: Our lives are filled with both good and bad, sources of both joy and struggle. Although this is the inevitable nature of life, where we choose to bring our focus and awareness is crucial, and has significant implications for our mental health and happiness. Indeed, no matter how difficult of a time we might be going through, there are always people or things in our lives that we can feel thankful for. Some of these may seem quite small or insignificant, while others may be more profound. Reflecting back over the past week, please write down five things that you feel thankful or grateful for. Once you've done so, briefly reflect and write down how doing so makes you feel. For the next eight weeks, complete this exercise at least once per week.

Example:

Gratitude #1: I feel thankful for my health. Although I've been struggling with a back injury, I feel fortunate that my overall health is good and that I'm still able to do most things that I'm passionate about.

Gratitude #2: I feel grateful for my wife. She has been incredibly patient and supportive of me as I've been writing this book, and always keeps me grounded.

Gratitude #3: I feel grateful that I've had the opportunity to travel. I love getting to experience other cultures and lands, and I feel so lucky that my job permits me the financial ability and flexibility to travel.

Gratitude #4: I feel thankful that my car works. I can remember times in my life when money was very tight, and I'd cross my fingers each day hoping that my car would start.

Gratitude #5: I am thankful for having good colleagues, who help make my job both rewarding and fun.

Reflection: Doing this exercise, I notice myself feeling surprised at how some of the things I can take for granted (like having a working car) can truly be a source of deep gratitude. And even aspects of my life that can sometimes cause me stress (like work, or my health) can similarly be a real source of thankfulness. When I really focus on these positive aspects of my life, I notice myself feeling calmer and more content hopeful about the future, and even feel better about myself.

Practice:

Gratitude #1:

_____

_____

_____

Gratitude #2:

_____

_____

_____

Gratitude #3:

_____

_____

_____

Gratitude #4:

_____

_____

_____

Gratitude #5:

_____

_____

_____

Reflection:

_____

_____

_____

Key Points to Consider:

✔ *Don't overdo it:* Research suggests that doing this exercise every day can actually be counterproductive (unlike the "Three Good Things" practice). This may be due to it feeling overly repetitive and thereby losing its impact. Instead, aim for journaling 1-3 times per week.

✔ *Don't worry about spelling or grammar:* Nobody has to see your gratitude journal except you, so have fun with it and don't sweat the small stuff.

✔ *Push your comfort zone:* If you notice yourself repeating many of the same things on your list (e.g. your spouse, your dog, etc.), take a moment to dig deeper. By doing so, you may be surprised how many sources of gratitude you have in your life.

✔ *Be sure to write it down:* Research suggests that in order to gain the full benefits from this exercise, it's important to take the time and write down your responses rather than simply reflecting on them.

How and Why It Works: The link between gratitude and well-being is one of the best-established in all the scientific literature. The cultivation of gratitude has been shown to potently counteract depression and anxiety, while fostering positive mood states. Moreover, high levels of gratitude are strongly associated with numerous physical health benefits. One of the best ways to begin tapping into the power of gratitude and harnessing its positive effects is through writing in a gratitude journal, like the one described above. By doing so, you'll begin noticing yourself appreciating positive aspects of your life, while putting the negative ones into better perspective.

Notes/Impressions:

_____

_____

_____

_____

_____

_____

_____

_____

_____

Your Inner "George Bailey"

. . . .

Duration: 20 minutes

Frequency: Flexible/as needed

Level of Difficulty: Moderate

Overview: The timeless holiday classic *It's a Wonderful Life* is not only a great movie, but also offers us some valuable clues about the importance of gratitude and how to best practice it. Without trying to give away too much, the film's protagonist (named George Bailey) becomes suicidal due to a setback, and decides to take his own life to help provide his family with a life insurance settlement. At this moment, he is rescued by a guardian angel named Clarence, who proceeds to take George on a whirlwind tour of what his world would look like had he never been born. George witnesses his brother passing away prematurely, his children never being born, his beloved hometown in shambles, and his beautiful wife struggling. In short, rather than simply asking George Bailey to reflect on what he was thankful for, Clarence did something altogether different: He showed George a world in which these blessings had never actually come to pass in the first place. Clarence's approach demonstrated to George just how special and extraordinary those gifts in fact were.

Although this sounds good in theory, and makes for a good movie, it begs a simple question: Does it actually work? It just so happens that two researchers were interested in whether this lesson from *It's a Wonderful Life* could help people in the real world. They decided to look specifically at married couples, and to explore the role of a specific type of gratitude exercise on marital satisfaction. One group of subjects was asked to simply write a brief story describing how they met their spouse. But the second group of subjects was instructed to write a brief story imagining what their life might look like had they never met their spouse. In other words, they were asked to tap into their inner "George Bailey." The results turned out to be quite surprising.

Although it might seem on the surface that the second exercise could perhaps be a bit of a downer, the findings from this study supported the exact opposite conclusion. In short, participants in the "George Bailey" condition ended up reporting that they felt significantly more satisfied in their relationship, along with feeling happier overall, than those in the control condition.

Why the difference? Timothy Wilson, one of research psychologists responsible for the study, stated that the exercise helped these relationships seem "surprising and special again, and maybe a little mysterious—the very conditions that prolong the pleasure we get from the good things in life." In other words, the "George Bailey" strategy seems to help turn things we might normally take for granted into something special once again.

Instructions: Take a moment and reflect on one person, opportunity, or experience in your life that brings you happiness or joy. This might be your spouse, a close friend, your job, your child, or something else altogether. Bask for a brief time in whatever feelings arise when you think about this part of your life, and notice whatever comes up for you. Think back to when, and under what circumstances, this good thing first entered your life. *Write this down:*

_____

_____

_____

Next, write down all the various ways in which this person or experience might have *never* come into your life in the first place. For example, if you met your spouse one day at a coffee shop, imagine all the ways in which that might not have occurred were it not for this fortunate timing. Expand your thinking, and reflect further on all the events and decisions, from the seemingly tiny to much more significant ones that could have happened differently to prevent this goodness from entering your life. *Write some of these thoughts:*

_____

_____

_____

Then, imagine what your life would be like today had it not been for this good fortune, and had this person or opportunity not entered your life. Reflect on the joys and feelings of happiness connected to this source of gratitude—and how this would all be missing from your life if it were absent. *Write some of these down:*

_____

_____

_____

Finally, bringing yourself back to the here and now, remind yourself that this person, opportunity, or experience is in fact a part of your life. Allow yourself to feel a deep sense of thankfulness and gratitude for their presence, and take a moment to savor how your life is better because of it. *Write any reactions to this:*

_____

_____

_____

Key Points to Consider:

✔ Try focusing on different areas of your life (e.g., interpersonal relationships, your career, experiences you cherish).

✔ Some people find that having a consistent time to practice this skill helps to turn it into a habit. You might find that doing it, for example, each weekend can set a good tone for the coming week.

✔ Experiment with frequency. There's no hard and fast rule for how often or rarely to engage in this practice, so play around with it to find the right balance for you.

How and why it works: Although different from many other gratitude techniques, the "George Bailey" technique has been shown to have powerful effects on our happiness and life satisfaction. Many of us find it all too easy to take positive aspects of our lives for granted, particularly as time goes on. This practice helps to counteract this tendency, and to help us gain greater appreciation for the good things in our lives. Indeed, by imagining the absence of these good things, we can gain even greater thankfulness for their presence.

Notes/Impressions:

_____

_____

_____

_____

_____

Reflecting on Hardship

• •

Duration: 10-15 minutes

Frequency: Flexible/as needed

Level of Difficulty: Moderate

Overview: Most gratitude techniques are aimed at developing greater appreciation for the good things in our lives. But some research suggests that a useful way to increase appreciation for our present circumstances can come from consciously and deliberately reflecting back on periods of hardship or struggle. Gratitude expert Robert Emmons has referred to this sort of practice as "remembering the bad." His findings suggest that by consciously thinking back to these more difficult periods in life, we can create fertile ground for gratitude to spring forth. This can be a particularly powerful strategy during periods of high stress or struggle, when it can be difficult to get in touch with feelings of gratitude and easy to lose sight of the goodness in our lives.

Instructions: Take a moment and reflect on a difficult period in your life, a time in which you struggled with pain, hardship, or heartache. It can be a time in the relatively recent past, or a much more distant time. Remember the feelings of sadness or even despair that you fought during this darkest of hours. Try to be as specific as possible in recalling a particular memory that comes to mind. *Notice the various thoughts, memories, images, and emotions that spring forth for you in this moment, and write down some of what comes up for you:*

_____

_____

_____

_____

_____

_____

Now returning to the present moment, remember that no matter what occurred back then, you were able to overcome that suffering and be here today. Even the worst of times are merely temporary, and you have within you the strength to survive and live on. The fact that you are here today, able to remember these difficult moments, is testimony to your strength and perseverance. Having grounded yourself in this realization, take a moment to reflect on anything that comes up. How has reflecting on difficulties in the past changed your perspective towards today? Are you able to look at your present circumstances in a different light? *Write down anything that comes up for you in doing this exercise:*

_____

_____

_____

_____

_____

Key Points to Consider:

✔ Whereas most gratitude practices focus on good things that exist in our present circumstances, this practice focuses instead on difficult experiences in the past, which can put our present circumstances in a new light.

✔ When getting started with this practice, don't start off with reflecting on the absolute most painful period in your past, as this can be overwhelming. Instead, begin by reflecting on moderately difficult periods from the past, and work your way up.

✔ Although simply reflecting on these times in our lives can be powerful, research suggests that taking the time to write them down makes the exercise that much more potent.

How and why it works: Most of us occasionally fall prey to losing sight of the good elements of our lives, or taking for granted various sources of gratitude that might be present for us. This is very natural, but can also make it difficult for us to feel fulfilled and happy. By consciously turning our attention to difficult times in the past, we can gain greater appreciation for the positive aspects of our present circumstances. For example, if we can reflect on times when we didn't have a working car, struggled to put food on the table, were out of a job, and so forth, doing so can make us appreciate the good things that happened so much more.

Notes/Impressions:

_____

_____

_____

_____

_____

_____

_____

_____

_____

A Day of Thanks

. . . .

Duration: Variable

Frequency: Weekly or monthly, as desired

Level of Difficulty: Easy/Moderate

Overview: The practice of gratitude is often by nature a very interpersonal endeavor. When we are grateful, we first recognize that our lives are filled with good fortune. But secondly, we recognize and acknowledge that the source of this goodness comes from outside of us. Indeed, we often have other people to thank for good things that we experience and encounter in life.

In this practice, you'll be working on both acknowledging the good things that come your way, but also directly communicating your gratitude to others who helped make these things possible. Choose one day out of the week or month to serve as your "day of thanks," and allow it to give you a regular dose of gratitude in your life.

Instructions: Throughout our lives, we are often on the receiving end of kindness from others, ranging from those closest to us to even strangers. Over the course of the next week (or month, if you prefer), choose one day to serve as your day of "thanks-giving." On that day, go out of your way to express gratitude to anyone and everyone who treats you with kindness, even for seemingly small acts. Whether it's a person holding the door for you, or someone who simply asks how you are doing, go out of your way to verbally express your gratitude towards them. Use the following space below to write about your experience.

Day/Date of my "Day of Thanks:" _____

Who I thanked over the course of the day:

_____

_____

_____

What it was like to express gratitude in this way:

_____

_____

_____

How and why it works: Acknowledging all that we are grateful for is crucial to happiness and well-being. But expressing these feelings directly to people around us can both bolster these positive emotions as well as strengthen our interpersonal relationships, which is another key component of lasting well-being.

Notes/Impressions:

_____

_____

_____

_____

_____

_____

_____

_____

A Meditation on Gratitude

. . . .

Duration: 10 minutes

Frequency: As needed

Level of Difficulty: Easy

Overview: The practice of gratitude has been linked with a host of benefits to our mental and physical health, including higher levels of happiness, reduced rates of depression and anxiety, and even better sleep and immune functioning. But while our lives are filled with good things, it can oftentimes be difficult to "hold onto" these sources of gratitude in the midst of everyday stress and worry. This practice invites you to combine the power of gratitude and meditation, to help you savor the good things in your life.

Instructions: Begin this practice by finding a comfortable, peaceful place to sit. As you're beginning this practice, try setting aside around 10 minutes per day to start off with, though you can of course extend this further in the days to come. Keep your back straight, allowing your shoulders to relax. Feel free to close your eyes, or if you prefer, choose a spot in front of you to rest your gaze softly upon.

1. Start off by taking three gentle and easy breaths, allowing your breath to come in and out through your nostrils. With each successive breath, feel yourself slowing down ever so slightly and becoming more connected to the moment.

2. You may notice your mind wandering, or your thoughts drifting throughout this practice, which it totally normal. Simply notice this tendency of the mind to wander, and gently return your attention and awareness to your breath.

3. For a few more minutes, continue to breathe slowly and evenly. Notice what's happening in your mind and in your body without judgment, and without wishing for anything to be different than it is right here and right now. Each time your mind takes you elsewhere, simply bring your awareness back to your breath.

4. When you are ready, try to identify someone or something in your life that you are feeling particularly thankful for in this moment. It can be another person, a beloved pet, a recent turn of good fortune, or anything else that is positive in your life. Try to be specific, and take a moment to get in touch with this blessing.

5. In your mind's eye, paint in all the mental details associated with this source of gratitude. Really get in touch with it, and allow the positive emotions to pour over you in this moment. Each time your mind wanders or your attention drifts, redirect it back to this feeling of gratitude.

6. Spend the next few minutes allowing yourself to bask in this feeling of thanks. Draw it out, and feel the bounty of good fortune in your life. If other positive sources of gratitude emerge, allow those to enter as well. Feel your heart open up, letting in these feelings of warmth and thankfulness.

7. After 10 minutes have passed, slowly and gently open your eyes and bring your awareness back to your surroundings.

How and why it works: Although studies suggest that most people experience more good things than bad on average, negative experiences have a much more powerful impact on our minds and bodies due to our brain's built-in negativity bias. Because of this, it's important for happiness that we learn to draw out positive experiences and really get in touch with them on a deeper level. This gratitude meditation can be a powerful practice to help us identify sources of gratitude in our lives, and to fully let them in on an emotional level.

Notes/Impressions:

_____

_____

_____

_____

_____

_____

_____

_____

The Gratitude Jar

. . . .

Duration: 1-5 minutes per day

Frequency: Daily—repeat for either 1 month or 1 year

Level of Difficulty: Easy/Moderate

Overview: The practice of gratitude has been linked with a host of benefits to our mental and physical health, including higher levels of happiness, reduced rates of depression and anxiety, and even better sleep and immune functioning. But in the midst of day-to-day life, it can sometimes be difficult to consciously call to mind the things we are grateful for. This practice invites you to write down one source of gratitude every day, and place the note in a jar (or similar container). At the end of a month (or a year if you prefer), empty your jar and re-experience all these sources of joy in your life.

Instructions: At the end of each day, write down one thing you are thankful for and place your note in a jar. It can be something that went well that day, or a more general source of gratitude. Repeat this practice for either one month, or if you prefer, one year. At the end of whichever time period you choose, set aside a nice chunk of time to empty your jar and read through your various notes. Take your time to fully savor and relive these positive experiences, picturing them in your mind and feeling whatever emotions come up for you as you do. Realize that your life is filled with many good things, with more to come. *Once you've read through your notes and taken it all in, write down any reactions that come up for you:*

_____

_____

_____

_____

_____

_____

How and why it works: Creating a "Gratitude Jar" can be a powerful experience for several reasons. First, it enables us to identify something we are grateful for each day, reinforcing the habit of gratitude. Next, when we empty our jar and reflect on all the sources of gratitude from the previous month (or even year), we are struck by how filled our lives are with goodness and sources of thankfulness.

Notes/Impressions:

_____

_____

_____

_____

_____

_____

_____

_____

CHAPTER 3

Kindness and Compassion

> *If you want to be happy, practice compassion.*
>
> —His Holiness, the Dalai Lama

> *Three things in human life are important: the first is to be kind; the second is to be kind; and the third is to be kind.*
>
> —Henry James

What Is Kindness and Compassion?

Kindness and compassion are two distinct yet interconnected concepts, both of which have been shown to have tremendous benefits to our psychological and physical health. They can be loosely defined as follows:

- *Kindness*: Doing something for the benefit of another, with no direct measurable or material benefit to ourselves.
- *Compassion*: Literally means "to suffer with," and is considered to mean the ability to experience the emotions of another person coupled with a desire to alleviate their suffering.

Both kindness and compassion have been linked to many positive outcomes, including higher levels of happiness and well-being, improved physical health, longevity, and lower levels of depression and anxiety.

Why Practice Kindness and Compassion?

The past decade or so has marked an explosion of research on the many benefits of kindness and compassion. As it turns out, practicing acts of kindness and becoming a more compassionate person is not only a worthy goal in and of itself; doing so is good *for* us as well.

The Psychological Benefits of Compassion and Kindness

Studies show that individuals who engage in acts of kindness, and who foster a sense of compassion toward others, perform better across a number of areas pertaining to mental and emotional health. The research-backed benefits include (but are not limited to) lower rates of depression and anxiety, higher levels of happiness and well-being, an enhanced sense of meaning and purpose, and improved recovery from alcohol and substance use issues.

The Health Benefits of Compassion and Kindness

Not only are compassionate individuals happier, research suggests that they are healthier as well. Studies have found that individuals who regularly practice compassion and kindness have improved overall physical health, stronger immune systems, and reduced rates of stress-related illnesses. Some research suggests that their lifespans are drastically longer as well, even among people struggling with chronic illnesses.

The Interpersonal Benefits of Kindness and Compassion

Numerous studies have linked the practices of kindness and compassion to stronger interpersonal relationships, including enhanced romantic relationships. In addition, some research suggests that compassionate individuals perform better at the workplace as well, and are more likely to gain promotions and even earn more money.

Your Brain on Compassion

Engaging in kindness and compassion is believed to impact our brain and body in a number of ways. First, on a structural level, the practice of compassion has been linked to the activation of the pleasure centers of our brain; in fact, studies show that the same regions of our brain that become active when we receive a gift become active when we give to others. Additionally, engaging in kindness and compassion has been shown to activate specific regions of our prefrontal cortex that are associated with emotion regulation and emotional processing. Some research even suggests that engaging in acts of kindness and compassion helps to stimulate our vagus nerve, which is linked to feelings of calm, connectedness, and tranquility.

On a chemical level, the practice of compassion has been linked to increased activation of dopamine and endorphins, which may help explain the feeling of a "warm glow" or mild euphoria you might often feel when you see the direct impact of your kindness on others in your life.

Five Acts of Kindness

. . . .

Duration: Flexible

Frequency: One day per week, for four weeks

Level of Difficulty: Moderate

Overview: Engaging in kindness towards others is an inherently rewarding experience. But recent research suggests that in addition to helping the individual on the receiving end, kindness and compassion has the power to transform our physical and emotional well-being. In fact, recent findings suggest that doing so is one of the most powerful and predictable ways to lastingly increase our own happiness. This exercise invites you to tap into this by engaging in small, everyday acts of giving towards others.

Instructions: In our everyday lives, we all perform acts of kindness towards others, and receive similar kindness from others as well. Some of these acts may be smaller in scale, while others are larger in scope. Sometimes, the person on the receiving end of our kindness may not even be aware of the act. Examples of these everyday acts of kindness include volunteering at a local community agency, donating blood, helping a friend paint a house, bringing coffee to a colleague, or feeding the parking meter for a stranger.

In the coming week, choose a single day to serve as your "kindness day." On that day, perform five acts of kindness towards others, and repeat this practice for at least four weeks. As you do so, I recommend keeping a small journal to help you keep track of the kind acts you engage in, as well as the emotional impact they have on you. This helps you to maintain accountability as you engage in the practice and learn more about the effect that giving to others has on your own emotional well-being.

Example:

Kindness Day: Tuesday, November 11th

Kind Act #1: This morning, I brought coffee for the support staff at work.

Kind Act #2: I donated a small bit of money to a charitable organization.

Kind Act #3: Today, I held the door for the first five people entering our clinic and wished them a good day.

Kind Act #4: This evening, I sent a message checking in on a friend I haven't seen in a few years, asking how they are doing.

Kind Act #5: Today, I tracked down and thanked a colleague who had helped me last week.

Impressions/Experience: Performing these small acts of kindness felt good in the moment, and even turned out to be fun. Doing them also made me feel better about myself, and more connected to people around me. I especially liked the ones that brought me face-to-face with other people, so that I could directly see the impact that my actions had on them.

Practice:

Kindness Day (Date):

_____

_____

_____

Kind Act #1:

_____

_____

_____

Kind Act #2:

_____

_____

_____

Kind Act #3:

_____

_____

_____

Kind Act #4:

_____

_____

_____

Kind Act #5:

_____

_____

_____

Impressions/Experience:

_____

_____

_____

Key Points to Consider:

✔ Don't worry about scale or scope.

✔ Try "bunching up" your kind acts: Some research shows that engaging in a handful of small acts of kindness on a single day is actually more effective than doing one act of kindness per day spread out over the course of the week.

✔ Get personal: When we practice acts of kindness directly, we receive an even greater boost to our happiness and well-being.

✔ Get some variety: Try varying how and when you engage in kind acts, so that it doesn't start to feel routine or rote.

How and why it works: Practicing kindness and compassion towards others helps us in several ways. First, it provides us with a sense of connection to those around us, and boosts our feelings of self-worth and meaning. Furthermore, there is evidence that engaging in kindness and compassion activates the pleasure and reward circuits of our brain, and may even lead to a release of both dopamine and endorphins. Another benefit of kindness is that it helps us view our own struggles in a different light, and offers us a new perspective on our own troubles. By engaging in even small acts of kindness, such as the ones encouraged in this exercise, you'll begin to experience some of the many benefits to our mental and physical health.

Notes/Impressions:

_____

_____

_____

_____

_____

_____

_____

_____

Better to Give Than to Receive?

. . . .

Duration: Flexible

Frequency: One time; repeat as desired

Level of Difficulty: Moderate

Overview: We've heard the age-old adage that "it's better to give than to receive." Although it's a nice sentiment, there was little known for many years whether this notion was true from a scientific perspective. Recent research suggests that in fact it is. Indeed, in terms of both emotional and physical health, the benefit of giving to others exceeds the benefit of receiving. In this exercise, you'll be putting this theory to the test in your own life, as you explore what it's like to give versus receive kindness.

Instructions: Over the next week, choose one activity to engage in that's purely for personal pleasure or fun, and one that's for the benefit of someone else. To make for a fair comparison, try choosing two activities that are roughly similar in terms of their time commitment and the effort required. For example, we wouldn't want to compare going to the Super Bowl (a pleasurable activity for many) with buying a friend a cup of coffee.

At the end of the week, once you've completed each of these activities, set aside some time to journal about the experience. To help you get started, feel free to use the following questions as prompts to guide your reflection:

1. What were the two activities that you engaged in? What did you do for yourself, and what did you do for another person?
2. How did it feel doing the pleasurable or fun activity? What emotions were most prominent as you engaged in it?
3. How did it feel doing the activity for someone else? What emotions were most prominent for you?
4. What differences did you notice in terms of how it felt to engage in these two activities?
5. Did either one seem to have a longer, more potent, or more powerful effect? If so, which one seemed to have this impact?
6. Did you learn anything, or notice anything surprising, as a result of doing this experience?

_____

_____

Key Points to Consider:

✔ Most people who complete this exercise find both activities to be enjoyable, but many find that the positive feelings from the second one tend to stick with them longer.

✔ As mentioned in the instructions, try to make sure that the two activities you choose are roughly equivalent in terms of their time commitment and effort required.

✔ Try to get personal: As with many practices, some research suggests that engaging in acts of kindness face-to-face can yield an even greater impact on our happiness and well-being.

How and why it works: Practicing kindness and compassion towards others helps us in a number of ways. First, it provides us with a sense of connection to those around us, and boosts our feelings of self-worth and meaning. Furthermore, there is evidence that engaging in kindness and compassion activates the pleasure and reward circuits of our brain, and may even lead to a release of both dopamine and endorphins. Another benefit of kindness is that it helps us view our own struggles in a different light, and offers us a new perspective on our own troubles. This exercise helps you compare and contrast what it's like to engage in a more purely pleasurable activity versus one that involves giving to others.

Notes/Impressions:

_____

_____

_____

_____

_____

_____

_____

Volunteering for a Cause

. . . .

Duration: Flexible

Frequency: Flexible

Level of Difficulty: Flexible

Overview: One of the most powerful and scientifically-validated steps we can take towards happiness is to engage in volunteer work. Recent research in the field of well-being has shown some of the many benefits associated with getting involved in volunteering. Among these are lower rates of overall stress, increased happiness and life satisfaction, a deeper sense of meaning and purpose, and even a longer lifespan. This next practice invites you to tap into the powerful benefits of volunteering. Remember, it doesn't take a huge time commitment in order to reap the many benefits stemming from volunteering. Even committing to doing one to two hours every few months can be sufficient in giving us a deeper sense of meaning and purpose while boosting our overall happiness level.

Instructions: Volunteering our time in the service of others has been shown to be one of the most powerful paths to increasing our own happiness as well as improving our physical health. But with so many potential avenues out there to volunteer, it can be daunting knowing where to start. One of the most important steps we can take is to begin identifying what matters to us, and what sort of role we wish to play in working towards that cause. To help you get started, use the following questions to get your creative juices flowing:

1. **Passions:** *What types of issues, causes, or subjects seem to stoke your passions or rouse your interests?*

   _____

   _____

   _____

2. **Skills:** What sorts of abilities or skills do you possess that you can tap into in the service of others?

_____

_____

_____

3. **Needs:** What kind of demand is out there for the issues that you're passionate about?

_____

_____

_____

4. **Scale and scope:** Do you prefer being involved in a larger cause, including worldwide issues such as international aid or the environment? Or might you prefer to be more connected to a cause closer to your community?

_____

_____

_____

5. **Time:** How much of yourself do you feel able to give at this point in time? Do you want to start off engaging in a one-time opportunity (like a park cleanup), or would you prefer something that's more ongoing (like tutoring, or a Big Brother-type program)?

_____

_____

_____

Once you've had the chance to brainstorm potential interests, begin exploring ways that you can match those interests to existing opportunities to volunteer. Two great places to start include:

- www.volunteermatch.com
- www.serve.gov

After you've had the chance to engage in a volunteer opportunity, I highly recommend journaling about the experience. Take some time to reflect on what the experience was like for you, the impact that it had on your mood, and how you felt both during and after.

Key Points to Consider:

✔ Give what you can: Be honest with yourself about how much time and effort you feel able to commit. Remember, don't overcommit and then set yourself up for feeling overwhelmed or resentful afterwards. A little bit can certainly go a long way when it comes to volunteer work.

✔ Connect to a cause you believe in: If you can identify an opportunity that aligns with your values and really matters to you, it's likely to feel even more fulfilling and make you want to continue building on your initial experience.

✔ Make it social: Engaging in volunteer work with a loved one or a friend can make it even more fun, and make you even more likely to repeat it in the future.

How and why it works: Practicing kindness and compassion towards others helps us in a number of ways. First, it provides us with a sense of connection to those around us, and boosts our feelings of self-worth and meaning. Furthermore, there is evidence that engaging in kindness and compassion activates the pleasure and reward circuits of our brain, and may even lead to a release of both dopamine and endorphins. Another benefit of kindness is that it helps us view our own struggles in a different light, and offers us a new perspective on our own troubles. This exercise helps you to experience first-hand the incredible benefits associated with volunteering. Best of all, unlike donating to a cause from afar, volunteer work tends to be very hands-on and face-to-face, which yields even bigger benefits from a happiness and well-being perspective.

Notes/Impressions:

_____

_____

_____

_____

Recalling Kindness Towards Others

. . . .

Duration: 15 minutes

Frequency: Weekly

Level of Difficulty: Moderate

Overview: Although the majority of kindness-oriented practices involve engaging in new acts of compassion towards others, some research suggests that it may be equally important for us to step back and appreciate the ways in which we already show kindness and compassion. In other words, instead of simply expanding the ways in which we practice kindness towards others, it is just as critical that we pause and acknowledge the ways in which we are already doing so.

Instructions: In our everyday lives, we all practice acts of compassion and kindness to those around us. At times, we do this without much conscious awareness, perhaps because it comes easily to us and we give it little thought. Recent findings in the field of happiness and well-being research suggests that it can be very helpful to step back, notice, and savor the ways in which we are already helping others in our life.

Thinking back over the past week, reflect on the ways in which you've already shown kindness towards others, or helped someone in need. These acts of kindness may be seemingly small ones, such as holding the door for someone, or offering a friendly smile to a stranger; or they may be more significant in nature, such as volunteering at a local agency, or mowing the lawn for an elderly couple that lives down the street. No matter the size of the act, reflect on the ways in which you have shown kindness and compassion toward others over the past week. Write down five such examples, and repeat on a weekly basis.

Example:

Kind Act #1: Called a friend to check in on how he was doing, because he'd been struggling recently.

Kind Act #2: Put money in a stranger's parking meter that had just expired.

Kind Act #3: Paid for a stranger's coffee who had forgotten their wallet.

Kind Act #4: Sent a "get well" card to someone who'd been battling a health problem.

Kind Act #5: Covered a hospital shift for a colleague who was feeling overwhelmed with responsibilities at work.

Practice:

Kind Act #1:

_____

_____

_____

Kind Act #2:

_____

_____

_____

Kind Act #3:

_____

_____

_____

Kind Act #4:

_____

_____

_____

Kind Act #5:

_____

_____

_____

Key Points to Consider:

✔ Feel free to experiment with frequency; some people enjoy looking back one week at a time, while others prefer to check in with themselves at the end of each day to add to their list.

✔ Notice the small stuff: Many seemingly smaller acts of kindness can go unnoticed, so take a moment and reflect on all the ways you've shown compassion and kindness towards others.

✔ Allow it to sink in: After generating your list of kind acts, take a moment to savor the positive feelings that come up for you after reflecting on them.

How and why it works: Practicing kindness and compassion towards others helps us in a number of ways. First, it provides us with a sense of connection to those around us, and boosts our feelings of self-worth and meaning. Furthermore, there is evidence that engaging in kindness and compassion activates the pleasure and reward circuits of our brain, and may even lead to a release of both dopamine and endorphins. Another benefit of kindness is that it helps us view our own struggles in a different light, and offers us a new perspective on our own troubles. It can be easy to overlook the ways in which we are already engaging in acts of compassion and altruism, particularly in small ways. This exercise helps you to identify the various ways that kindness and compassion are already a part of your everyday life.

Notes/Impressions:

_____

_____

_____

_____

_____

_____

The Gift of Time

. . . .

Duration: Flexible

Frequency: As needed

Level of Difficulty: Moderate

Overview: From the food we eat, to the way in which we communicate with one another, our world continues to trend towards brevity and efficiency at a staggering pace. With it, our fast-paced world seems to grow faster still with each passing day. Although some of these developments have led to positive changes, they bring costs with them as well. Whereas previous generations were marked by close, face-to-face interpersonal interactions, today it can seem that the extent of our interactions can be summed up in e-mails, "tweets," and text messages.

Though harmless on the surface, this lack of true interpersonal connectivity has profound negative impacts on our mental and physical health, and has even been linked to rising rates of mental illness. Just as the "slow food" movement has come to be viewed as an antidote of sorts to our fast food culture, so too do we need an antidote for the fast-paced, increasingly impersonal world we live in. To foster true happiness and lasting well-being, it is imperative that we connect interpersonally in a genuine way. This holds particularly true when those we care about are struggling or suffering. Indeed, during times of need, there is often no greater cure than a sense of true connection, caring and compassion; this exercise invites you to do just that.

Instructions: For this act of kindness and compassion, reflect on someone in your life who may be going through a hard time, or has been struggling in some way. Perhaps it's a friend, a parent, a loved one, or a co-worker. If geographically possible, try scheduling a time in the coming week to spend time with this individual. Get together with this individual, and offer him or her some much-needed support face-to-face. Block out a sizable chunk of your day, turn off your cell phone, and try to be as present as possible for this person. Afterwards, reflect on what the experience was like for you, and how this small act of kindness seemed to impact this other person.

How and why it works: Most people who complete this practice find that its personal touch brings about substantial feelings of warmth and connection, and can help strengthen interpersonal bonds. This can be particularly powerful because just as compassion holds many benefits to our happiness, the same holds true of fostering close interpersonal connections.

Notes/Impressions:

_____

_____

_____

_____

_____

_____

_____

_____

_____

CHAPTER 4

Mindfulness

> *The present moment is filled with joy and happiness; if you are attentive, you will see it.*
>
> —Thich Nhat Hanh

What Is Mindfulness?

We spend much of our lives on autopilot, aimlessly shifting from task to task, with little conscious awareness of where we are, or what we're doing. For example, we drive to and from work, with little memory of the actual experience. Or we eat a meal, and it's gone before we know it. These experiences are quite common, and are the hallmark of mindlessness. In fact, one notable study found that we spend nearly half our waking hours in this sort of state. Worse yet, we tend to be most unhappy during these periods when our mind is wandering.

The antidote to this state of mindlessness is in fact *mindfulness*, an ancient practice that's only more recently come to be understood and appreciated by modern science. In a nutshell, mindfulness refers to:

- Maintaining moment-to-moment awareness of our thoughts, feelings, sensations, and surrounding environment.
- Practicing acceptance of these experiences without judgment, meaning we observe what's happening around and within us, without wishing for them to be any different than they are.

Why Practice Mindfulness?

The past decade has seen a surge of research on the many benefits of mindfulness. As it turns out, the practice of mindfulness has been linked to a host of positive outcomes, including improved psychological health, enhanced physical well-being, and even improved interpersonal relationships and job performance.

The Psychological Benefits of Mindfulness

Studies show that individuals who regularly practice mindfulness perform better across a number of areas when it comes to mental and emotional health. For example, people who practice mindfulness have been found to have lower rates of depression, stress, and anxiety, while having higher rates of happiness, well-being, and positive emotional states. Additionally, mindfulness has been linked to improved memory, concentration, and focus, along with enhanced problem-solving skills and creativity.

The Health Benefits of Mindfulness

Not only are mindful individuals happier, research suggests that they are healthier as well. Studies have found that individuals who regularly practice mindfulness have better overall physical health, require fewer hospital visits, and spend fewer days in the hospital than their less mindful peers. Additionally, they have stronger immune systems, and have been found to be better equipped to combat chronic illnesses. Some studies have even found that mindfulness practice has been linked to lower levels of physical pain, even among patients with chronic pain.

The Interpersonal Benefits of Mindfulness

Individuals who practice mindfulness reap a number of rewards beyond their physical and mental health. For example, interventions examining mindfulness in schools have found that students who practice mindfulness are less prone to behavioral problems and have higher rates of achievement. Furthermore, in studies of workplace success, researchers have linked mindfulness to higher rates of both job performance and job retention. Finally, studies examining the impact of mindfulness on relationships have found that mindfulness practice is strongly linked to closer interpersonal relationships, including enhanced romantic relationships.

The Mindful Brain

The practice of mindfulness is believed to impact our brain in multiple ways. On a structural level, the practice of mindfulness has been linked to increased activation in the left prefrontal cortex, a part of our brain connected to positive emotional states. Additionally, practicing mindfulness over time has been connected to decreased activation in the amygdala, an area of the brain implicated in our fight-or-flight and stress responses.

Furthermore, regions of our brain pertaining to memory, learning, and emotion regulation have all been linked to the practice of mindfulness as well. A recent study conducted on individuals who regularly engaged in mindfulness practice has also found that mindfulness helps slow down a process known as "cortical thinning," which refers to the process in which we slowly lose brain cells as we age.

Mindful Breathing

. . . .

Duration: 10 minutes

Frequency: Flexible

Level of Difficulty: Moderate

Overview: Many of us find our minds constantly wandering throughout the day. At times we may obsess over what's to come in the future, or ruminate about events from the past. Some studies even suggest that the average person's mind wanders nearly half of our waking hours. Worse yet, the more this happens, the greater our suffering seems to be. Given this, it's crucial to increase our ability to be in contact with the present moment in order to cultivate greater happiness and well-being. To do so, it helps to have an anchor to the present, and our breath serves as a perfect instrument to help us with this. Indeed, our breath is with us each moment of each day, from the moment we're born. Yet much of the time, it operates outside our conscious awareness. By consciously and deliberately focusing on our breath, we can slowly over time cultivate our ability to be mindful, and thus enhance our well-being.

Instructions: Begin this practice by finding a comfortable, peaceful place to sit. As you're beginning this practice, try setting aside around 10 minutes per day to start off with, though you can of course extend this further as you wish in the days to come. Keep your back straight, allowing your shoulders to relax. Feel free to close your eyes, or if you prefer, choose a spot in front of you to rest your gaze softly on.

1. Start off by taking three gentle and easy breaths, allowing your breath to come in and out through your nostrils. With each successive breath, feel yourself slowing down ever so slightly and becoming more connected to this moment.

2. You may notice your mind wandering, or your thoughts drifting throughout this practice, which is totally normal. Simply notice this tendency of the mind to wander, and gently return your attention and awareness to your breath.

3. Bring full attention now to your breathing. Each time you inhale and exhale, observe where in your body you notice the breath most prominently. For some this may be in your chest, as it rises and falls with each breath. For others, this may be in the nostrils, as the air passes coolly on the way in, and slightly warmer on the way back out. Wherever it is, simply take a moment and notice where in your body you feel your breath the most.

4. Now take a moment and notice how it feels to focus fully on your inhale. As you inhale, observe any particular feelings of tension or strain, noticing the sensation of your lungs and abdomen filling up as you inhale.

5. After a few breaths, gently shift your awareness to focus more on your exhale. With each successive exhale, notice what it's like to feel your breath pass out through your nostrils. And continue to observe, without judgment, anything that you feel throughout your body.

6. For a few more minutes, continue to breathe slowly and evenly. Notice what's happening in your mind and in your body, without judgment, and without wishing for anything to be different than it is right here and right now. Each time your mind takes you elsewhere, simply bring your awareness back to your breath.

7. After 10 minutes have passed, gently open your eyes and bring your awareness back to your surroundings.

Key Points to Consider:

✔ Feel free to experiment with this exercise, to do it standing or seated, and at different times throughout the day.

✔ For those relatively new to mindfulness, this (and other mindfulness exercises) can feel quite challenging, and that's okay. Remember, cultivating greater present-moment awareness is a process, and can take time.

✔ Once you've developed this practice a bit, it can be a great stress-reducer during times of stress or anxiety.

How and why it works: Numerous studies have now shown the link between mindfulness and better overall health, reduced depression and anxiety, and greater ability to manage stress. One of the great benefits of mindfulness is that it enables us to gain greater distance from our negative thoughts and feelings, so that we don't feel overwhelmed by these difficult moments. By fully experiencing what's happening within us and around us, we can respond rather than simply react to life's stressors. Mindful breathing can be particularly helpful because it provides us with a built-in anchor to the present moment—our breath—that we can turn to no matter where we are. By spending more time in the present moment, and less time worrying about the past or the future, over time we can become both happier and healthier.

Notes/Impressions:

_____

_____

_____

Raisin Meditation

. . . .

Duration: 5-10 minutes

Frequency: Daily for one week

Level of Difficulty: Moderate

Overview: The cultivation of mindfulness can benefit us in countless ways, including improved physical health, enhanced psychological well-being, and closer interpersonal relationships. A remarkable power inherent within mindfulness is its ability to transform the mundane into something more incredible. Many of us find ourselves operating on "autopilot" much of the time, with little conscious awareness. Indeed, studies even show that our mind may be wandering nearly half of our waking hours. We drive to work, with little recollection of how we got there. We finish a meal, with little remembrance of how it tasted. These experiences are quite common, yet can also lead to negative physical and emotional consequences.

In this exercise, we'll harness the power of mindfulness to begin shifting from autopilot to conscious, present-moment awareness. To do so, we'll begin by focusing on an activity that all of us do every day: eating. But rather than trying to eat an entire meal in a mindful manner, we'll literally start with something much smaller—just a single raisin. To begin with, set aside around 10 minutes where you can do this exercise undisturbed. You'll need a few raisins for this practice, or if you prefer, any sort of small dried fruit (or even dark chocolate!).

Instructions: Begin this practice by setting aside 5 to 10 minutes in a quiet place, without distractions. Be sure to turn off your phone, shut off your television, and put aside anything else that might get in your way of being present. For the next few minutes, you'll be engaging in an activity that you do every day (eating), but approaching it in a vastly different manner than usual. Your task is to eat a raisin in a fully present, mindful manner.

1. Begin by taking a raisin and placing it in the palm of your hand. Gaze down at it, pretending for a moment that you've never seen this object before in your life. Notice the raisin in your hand, feeling its weight on your palm. After holding it in the palm of your hand for a few moments, place it between your forefinger and thumb to more fully feel its texture, and then once more return it to your palm.

2. Now take a few moments to fully see the raisin, really taking in the visual experience of the raisin in your palm. Notice the subtle details, its texture, its ridges, and its color. Notice the shadow it casts on your palm.

3. Place the raisin once more between your thumb and forefinger, noticing the texture even more fully. Bring it up to your nose, and gently inhale. See if you can detect any smells or scents; if you cannot, simply notice that as well.

4. When you are ready, slowly take the raisin and place it gently in your mouth, without yet taking a bite. Notice what happens within your mouth. You might notice yourself salivating a bit, or find your tongue "reaching out" towards the raisin. Whatever your experience is, simply take note of it.

5. Take a single bite of the raisin, piercing its skin and noticing the shift in flavors within your mouth. Notice the changes in texture as well. Continue to take a few more chews. Before swallowing, take a moment to fully notice and savor the experience.

6. Whenever you're ready, swallow the raisin, and continue to observe any thoughts, feelings, reactions, or emotions that come up for you as you do. Take a moment to sit with, and witness, whatever's happening within your mind and body.

Key Points to Consider:

✔ Although most studies have looked at using raisins for this exercise, there's nothing uniquely special about raisins. Indeed, feel free to use whatever you'd like for the purposes of this experiential exercise.

✔ If you find this difficult, remember that's totally okay! Most of us simply don't eat (or engage in most activities for that matter) in this sort of way. So be patient with yourself, and see where the experience takes you.

✔ Take your time. Try drawing this out, to more fully experience all the different sensations that you encounter while eating the raisin. Notice the different tastes, textures, and smells that come up for you.

How and why it works: Numerous studies have now shown the link between mindfulness and better overall health, reduced depression and anxiety, and greater ability to manage stress. One of the great benefits of mindfulness is that it enables us to gain greater distance from our negative thoughts and feelings, so that we don't feel overwhelmed by these difficult moments. By fully experiencing what's happening within us and around us, we can respond rather than simply react to life's stressors.

A great way to cultivate mindfulness is through consciously engaging in an activity we take part in every day—eating. Mindful eating allows us to immerse ourselves with the sensory experience of eating a raisin, which we can then use as a springboard to approach other daily activities in a different way.

Notes/Impressions:

_____

_____

_____

_____

_____

_____

_____

_____

_____

Everyday Mindfulness

. . . .

Duration: Flexible

Frequency: Daily for one week

Level of Difficulty: Moderate

Overview: As shown in the "raisin meditation," the practice of mindfulness can transform normal, everyday activities into something far more wondrous and meaningful. In this exercise, you are invited to take the lessons from the "raisin meditation" and apply them to other day-to-day experiences. Indeed, if we can turn the simple experience of eating a raisin into something profound, imagine what can be done for other areas of our lives.

Instructions: Begin by reflecting on a handful of activities that you engage in on a day-to-day basis, but which you often do in a "mindless" manner. Common examples of these may include (but are not limited to):

- Walking the dog
- Brushing your teeth
- Eating a meal
- Taking a shower
- Doing the dishes
- Driving to and from work
- Cleaning your home

For the next week, choose one of these activities to focus on each day. You don't have to change anything about your normal routine; rather, the idea is to instead change the way you experience it. When doing each activity, try using all of your senses to fully immerse yourself, rather than simply rushing onto the next thing or finding your mind drifting aimlessly. For example, while taking a shower, you might pay particular attention to the sensation of the water hitting your skin, the temperature of the water, the smell of the soap or shampoo, and so forth. Remember, it's normal and natural for our minds to wander off, and that's okay! Simply redirect your awareness each time to the experience you're focusing on. *At the end of the week, using either this space or a separate piece of paper, take a moment to write down any reflections or reactions you have regarding your experiences:*

_____

_____

_____

Key Points to Consider:

✔ Start with shorter activities as you get used to the practice, or break your activities up into smaller chunks. For example, if your commute to work takes an hour, don't worry about being "mindful" for the entire drive. Rather, commit to spending a shorter time period (even five minutes) in a more present manner.

✔ If your mind wanders off, that's totally okay! The most important thing is that we simply notice this happening, without judgment, and gently redirect our awareness back to the present.

How and why it works: Countless studies have shown the link between mindfulness and improved mental and physical health. Although formal meditation is a great way to cultivate the practice of mindfulness, it can be just as helpful to practice through more informal methods. There are numerous activities that we often engage in mindlessly, with our thoughts taking us just about anywhere except the present moment. In this exercise, you are invited to choose one such activity each day, and approach it in a different manner.

Notes/Impressions:

_____

_____

_____

_____

_____

_____

_____

Mindfulness of the Senses

· ·

Duration: 5-15 minutes

Frequency: Daily or as needed

Level of Difficulty: Moderate

Overview: The practice of mindfulness helps us to become more immersed in the present moment. Over time, the cultivation of mindfulness has been shown to have a multitude of benefits, including improved physical health, lower levels of depression and anxiety, lower stress, and greater levels of psychological well-being. One of the best ways to become more present is to increase our moment-to-moment awareness of our sensory experiences. In this exercise you'll begin practicing how to use your various senses (sight, touch, taste, smell, and hearing) to become more fully immersed in the present moment.

Instructions:

1. Begin by finding a comfortable, peaceful place to sit. Set aside around 10 minutes to start with when beginning this practice, though you can of course extend this time further in the days to come. Keeping your back straight, allow your shoulders to relax. Close your eyes if you're comfortable doing so; otherwise, choose a spot on the floor in front of you to softly focus your gaze.

2. Begin by taking three gentle and easy breaths, in and out of your nose, followed by slow and steady exhales. With each passing breath, feel yourself slowing down ever so slightly, and become more immersed in the moment.

3. If you notice your mind wandering or your thoughts drifting, simply notice this and return your awareness and attention to your breath. This may occur at many points throughout this meditation; it's simply what our mind does. Merely observe the tendency of your mind to wander, and without judgment, return your awareness to your breath.

4. Bring full attention now to your breathing. Notice the sensation of your breath as it enters and leaves your body. With each passing breath, observe yourself becoming more present in this moment.

5. When you're ready, bring your attention now to the sounds around you. Notice the sound of your breath as you slowly inhale in then exhale out. Notice even the faintest of sounds that you can

detect around you, and notice the silence as well. Imagine your ears as satellites, able to pick up on any and all sounds that surround you in this moment. Simply notice these sounds, without judgment, and without any desire for things to be different than they are.

6. Bring awareness now to any smells that you can detect. As you inhale, observe any scents, whether they are strong or faint, that your nose picks up. Observe any judgments that arise, and simply notice those as well. Take a few moments to fully observe any scents and smells that you can detect.

7. Shift your focus now to feeling your body, sitting in your chair or on the floor. Notice the weight of your body being supported beneath you. Become aware of the texture of the fabric of your clothing against your skin, the temperature of the air against your skin. Notice your hands, and feel them resting wherever they are placed. Take a few moments to fully notice all of this.

8. Now bring your awareness to any tastes that you can detect in your mouth. Whether faint or strong, simply observe any and all tastes that you're able to detect. If you're unable to, simply notice that as well.

9. With your eyes closed, imagine what the room looks like around you. Paint a picture in your mind's eye of what surrounds you right here in this moment. Try picturing the walls, the floor beneath you, and the colors of the room. Take a few moments to visualize your surroundings.

10. Now notice what's happening in your mind. Are your thoughts looking up ahead towards the future, backwards to the past, or are they here and now in the present moment? Without judgment, simply notice where your mind is taking you. If you catch your mind wandering or your thoughts drifting, don't judge yourself or react self-critically to this. Simply observe this, and gently redirect your attention and awareness back to your various senses.

11. After about 10 minutes have gone by, gently open your eyes, and bring your awareness back to your surroundings. Allow yourself to bask in the comfort and tranquility of the present moment for a few more moments.

Key Points to Consider:

✔ Feel free to experiment with this exercise, to do it standing or seated, and at different times throughout the day.

✔ For those relatively new to mindfulness, this (and other mindfulness exercises) can feel quite challenging, and that's okay. Remember, cultivating greater present-moment awareness is a process, and can take time.

✔ Once you've developed this practice a bit, it can be a great stress-reducer during times of stress or anxiety.

How and why it works: Numerous studies have shown the link between mindfulness and better overall health, reduced depression and anxiety, and greater ability to manage stress. One of the great benefits of mindfulness is that it enables us to gain greater distance from our negative thoughts and feelings, so that we don't feel overwhelmed by these difficult moments. By fully experiencing what's happening within us and around us, we can respond rather than simply react to life's stressors. Focusing on our various senses during mindfulness can be particularly helpful because it provides us with a built-in anchor to the present moment that we can turn to no matter where we are. By spending more time in the present moment, and less time worrying about the past or the future, we can over time become both happier and healthier.

Notes/Impressions:

_____

_____

_____

_____

_____

_____

_____

_____

A Mindful Minute

. . . .

Duration: One minute

Frequency: As needed

Level of Difficulty: Easy

Overview: Many of us find our minds constantly wandering throughout the day. Sometimes we may obsess over what's to come in the future, while at other points we may ruminate about events from the past. Research suggests that the average person's mind wanders nearly half of our waking hours. Worse yet, the more this happens, the greater our suffering seems to be. Given this, it's extremely important to increase our ability to be in contact with the present moment in order to cultivate greater happiness and well-being.

In our busy everyday lives, it can sometimes feel difficult to find the time to set aside even 10 or 15 minutes to practice mindfulness, let alone longer. For these occasions, it can help to take even just a few minutes to cultivate present-moment awareness through mindfulness. This practice invites you to tap into the power and promise of mindfulness in a single minute.

Instructions: In our busy world, it's incredibly important to take the time and slow down, and to become one with the present moment. Whenever you find yourself feeling stressed, try taking even a single minute to slow down and cultivate mindful awareness. Whether you are in the office or in your car, and whether you're sitting down or standing up, this practice can be done just about anywhere. All you need is a minute of silence. Feel free to close your eyes if you'd like, though you don't have to. For the next minute, put aside anything you are doing, and focus on the following:

1. Feel your breath come in and out through your nostrils. Feel it filling up your chest and lungs, and notice it as you exhale.
2. Use your senses to notice what's happening around you. Hear the sounds around you, feel the temperature of the air against your skin, and notice any smells, tastes, or textures.
3. Observe whatever emotions and thoughts are within you right in this moment. Simply notice these, without judgment and without any desire to change them.
4. Notice when your mind drifts, and bring it back each time to this moment.
5. When you're ready, open your eyes and come fully back.

How and why it works: Numerous studies have shown the link between mindfulness and better overall health, reduced depression and anxiety, and greater ability to manage stress. One of the great benefits of mindfulness is that it enables us to gain greater distance from our negative thoughts and feelings, so that we don't feel overwhelmed by these difficult moments. By fully experiencing what's happening within us and around us, we can respond rather than simply reacting to life's stressors. By spending more time in the present moment and less time worrying about the past or the future, we can over time become both happier and healthier. Even a brief mindfulness practice like this one can help us to slow down and become more present.

Notes/Impressions:

_____

_____

_____

_____

_____

_____

_____

_____

CHAPTER 5

Self-Compassion

> *If your compassion does not include yourself, it is incomplete.*
>
> —Jack Kornfield

> *Love yourself first, and everything else falls in line. You really have to love yourself to get anything done in this world.*
>
> —Lucille Ball

What Is Self-Compassion?

One of the world's foremost experts on self-compassion, psychologist Kristin Neff, has defined self-compassion as being comprised of three separate but interconnected parts:

- **Self-kindness:** The ability to treat ourselves with caring, kindness, and compassion, just as we would come to the aid of someone we care deeply about.
- **Common humanity:** The feeling of being connected with others, rather than feeling alone or isolated. Instead of viewing our problems and suffering as unique to us, we are able to remember that we are not alone.
- **Mindfulness:** Being able to accept and be aware of what we are experiencing, without trying to push it away or be overwhelmed by it.

Most of us tend to be harder on ourselves than we are on those around us, particularly those we care about. There are many roots to this tendency towards self-criticism, including childhood messages, societal expectations, and the belief that being hard on ourselves will somehow help us achieve goals and improve ourselves. However, in recent years the research has become clear: Self-criticism demoralizes us, and is actually hazardous to our mind and bodies. As an alternative, learning to be self-compassionate not only helps us to feel better emotionally, it also helps us achieve more professionally while also boosting our health.

Why Practice Self-Compassion?

The past decade or so has marked an explosion of research on the many benefits of self-compassion. By learning to relate to ourselves in a kinder, more compassionate manner, studies show that we can reap a host of rewards to our psychological and physical well-being.

The Psychological Benefits of Self-Compassion

Studies show that self-compassionate individuals have significantly lower rates of depression, anxiety, and stress, and are able to buffer themselves more effectively against future episodes of depression. There is also substantial evidence that self-compassion can help in the recovery from post-traumatic stress disorder, as well as individuals struggling with eating disorders. Finally, the practice of self-compassion has been shown to be helpful among individuals recovering from addiction issues.

The Health Benefits of Self-Compassion

Not only are self-compassionate individuals happier, research suggests that they are healthier as well. Studies have found that individuals who regularly foster self-compassion are better equipped to manage chronic pain, have healthier eating patterns, and are less likely to struggle with issues such as cigarette smoking and substance abuse. There is even evidence that self-compassion can help in the alleviation of chronic acne, in large part because it's a proven way to reduce stress levels in our bodies.

The Interpersonal Benefits of Self-Compassion

Self-compassionate individuals have stronger interpersonal relationships, including more satisfying romantic relationships, across a number of studies. They also are more likely to succeed both in school and at work, in large part because self-compassion helps us respond to setbacks and adversity in a more positive and productive manner.

Your Brain on Self-Compassion

The benefits of self-compassion are vast, but a closer look at what happens in our brains and bodies when we cultivate self-compassion sheds some light on its power. Before briefly discussing the impact of self-compassion on the brain, let's first explore what happens when we do the opposite and engage in self-criticism. When we self-criticize, our brain and body respond in a very specific manner. First, our amygdala becomes activated, which triggers our fight-or-flight and stress response. We also see increased blood pressure, along with the release of adrenaline and cortisol into our bloodstream.

When we practice self-compassion, a very different reaction occurs. First, there is decreased activation in the amygdala; instead, we see increased activation in the left prefrontal cortex (largely associated with positive emotional states) and the insula (associated with empathy). Moreover, rather than cortisol and adrenaline being released, self-compassion triggers the release instead of oxytocin, a hormone closely connected to love and bonding.

A Letter of Self-Compassion

. . . .

Duration: 15-20 minutes

Frequency: Repeat monthly or as needed

Level of Difficulty: Moderate

Overview: Many of us fall into a pattern of self-criticism in which we beat ourselves up because we feel as if we don't "measure up." Some studies even suggest that over 80% of people are harder on themselves than they are on others. There are many reasons for this, including internalized messages from childhood, adverse experiences throughout life, as well as societal beliefs around us. In this exercise, you'll begin harnessing the power of self-compassion through the experience of writing a letter of self-compassion. Because it's often easier to be kind towards others or to envision kindness coming from someone we care about, you'll be writing this letter from the standpoint of someone who cares (or cared) deeply for you.

Instructions: Before you start writing your letter, begin by reflecting on who in your life offers you compassion. It's often easier for us to offer kindness towards others, or to envision kindness being received from others, than it is to offer that compassion toward ourselves. So as you begin, start by identifying first a perceived flaw or shortcoming that you tend to beat yourself up over, and then see if you can identify a person in your life who you know cares genuinely and deeply for you.

Perceived flaw/shortcoming that I fixate on:

_____

_____

_____

Person in my life who shows me compassion:

_____

_____

_____

What words might this person say to me?

_____

_____

_____

What tone might they use in speaking to me?

_____

_____

_____

What actions might they take to convey caring and understanding?

_____

_____

_____

Once you've brainstormed a bit above, begin writing a draft of your letter. Don't worry about grammar, spelling, or format. Instead, simply allow yourself to explore the emotional reactions that come up for you, and see if you can tap into the felt sense of kindness and caring that would emanate from this individual. *Write your letter on a separate sheet of paper.*

Key Points to Consider:

✔ When you're identifying a perceived flaw that you'd like to be more self-compassionate about, it can help to start with something a bit "lighter." In other words, jumping right into your area of greatest insecurity or shame can feel overwhelming. Instead, begin by working on a less threatening part of your life.

✔ Don't worry about structure, format, or spelling. Just allow yourself to explore any emotions that arise in tapping into this felt sense of compassion toward yourself.

✔ Try taking it "to-go": Many people find it helpful to keep their self-compassion letter handy, so that they can turn to it when difficult feelings arise.

How and why it works: Many of us fall into patterns of self-criticism, in which we're much harder on ourselves than we would ever be towards others. Although we may believe this will help spur us to greater heights, the research is now fairly conclusive that self-criticism is connected to decreased levels of well-being and lower achievement. Conversely, self-compassion has been linked to numerous positive mental and physical health outcomes, including lower rates of depression and anxiety, and higher rates of happiness and well-being. This exercise helps us to begin this process of learning to be more self-compassionate towards ourselves. Over time and with practice, it can become a more deeply ingrained habit that can foster well-being.

Notes/Impressions:

_____

_____

_____

_____

_____

_____

_____

_____

Self-Compassion Break

· ·

Duration: Five minutes

Frequency: Daily, or as needed

Level of Difficulty: Easy/Moderate

Overview: As defined by experts such as Kristin Neff, self-compassion consists of three separate yet distinct ingredients:

- *Mindfulness:* Being aware of our pain, without pushing it away or overly identifying with it and letting it consume us.
- *Common Humanity:* The knowledge and understanding that we are not alone in our suffering, and that the experience of pain is indeed universal.
- *Self-Kindness:* Treating ourselves with caring and compassion.

In this exercise, you will be tapping into these three aspects of self-compassion and applying them to difficult experiences in your own life.

Instructions: First, reflect on a situation in your life that is causing you stress at this point in time. Try bringing it to mind, and allow yourself to feel the emotions associated with it. Notice what comes up for you. *Write down the source of this stress:*

_____

_____

_____

_____

_____

_____

Next, either out loud or in your mind, say to yourself, "This is a moment of pain and suffering." That's *mindfulness*—simply noticing what's happening in the present moment, without judgment. We're not trying to hold onto the pain too tightly, but we're also not trying to push it away. Conversely, you might say to yourself, "This is really stressful," or, "This hurts right now." Use whatever words and language feel right for you. *Write your statement tapping into mindful awareness:*

_____

_____

_____

_____

Next, silently or softly out loud, say to yourself, "Pain and suffering is an inevitable part of life." That's *common humanity*, the awareness that we all have experiences of suffering. Rather than feeling alone and isolated from those around us, common humanity helps us to recognize that everyone has moments of difficulty, struggle, and self-doubt. Conversely, you might say to yourself, "I'm not alone in this," or, "Everyone struggles sometimes." *Use whatever words feel natural to you, and in the space below write your statement of common humanity:*

_____

_____

_____

_____

Finally, gently say to yourself, "May I have kindness and compassion for myself." This is *self-kindness*, the belief that we too deserve compassion and caring when we're in pain. Conversely you might ask, "What do I need right now to care for myself," or say, "May I accept myself for who I am." Use whatever phrase or words feel right to you. ***When you're ready, use the space below to write your statement of self-kindness:***

_____

_____

_____

_____

_____

In the days to come, use this exercise to begin practicing how to respond with self-compassion during times of struggle. Although it may feel foreign at first, over time it will become more natural and instinctual. Use this practice at any time of day, wherever you are, to begin cultivating the valuable skill of self-compassion.

Key Points to Consider:

✔ In the beginning, practice this when you're feeling calm. Eventually it will be a great skill to turn to when difficult feelings arise, but when you're starting out, it can be easier to practice when you're feeling less emotional.

✔ Use whatever words feel natural to you. The suggestions above are simply examples—what's key is that you identify ways of relating to yourself that feel natural and congruent for you. So play around with it and experiment a bit.

How and why it works: Many of us fall into patterns of self-criticism, in which we're much harder on ourselves than we would ever be towards others. Although we may believe this will help spur us to greater heights, the research is now fairly conclusive that self-criticism is connected to decreased levels of well-being and lower achievement. Conversely, self-compassion has been linked to numerous positive mental and physical health outcomes, including lower rates of depression and anxiety, and higher rates of happiness and well-being.

This exercise helps us to begin the process of learning to be more self-compassionate towards ourselves. Because it can be done so briefly and occur almost anywhere, the "self-compassion break" is a great practice to tap into on an ongoing basis, so that we can turn to it during times of need. Over time and with practice, it can become a more deeply ingrained habit that can foster well-being.

Notes/Impressions:

_____

_____

_____

_____

_____

_____

_____

_____

Loving-Kindness Meditation

. . . .

Duration: 10-20 minutes per day

Frequency: Daily or as needed

Level of Difficulty: Moderate

Overview: Loving-kindness meditation, also known as *Metta*, is a practice that dates all the way back to at least the fifth century. In contrast to some other forms of meditation, loving-kindness meditation is aimed specifically at cultivating a felt sense of interpersonal connection. Through words, emotions, and images, it has the potential to instill deep feelings of compassion, love, and happiness within us and towards those around us.

Though dating back nearly 1,500 years, interest in loving-kindness meditation has grown substantially over the past few years. Beyond public interest in it, researchers and academics have focused on it as well, and have discovered numerous health benefits including improved mental health, physical health, and even changes to the brain.

Instructions:

1. Begin by sitting in a comfortable position. Sit upright and relaxed, placing your hands gently on your lap. Start by taking three steady and even breaths. When you are ready, close your eyes.

2. Continue to breathe, slowly in and slowly out. Observe the feeling of the air entering through your nostrils, and notice how it's ever so slightly warmer on the way back out.

3. Become more aware of your body as you sit, and as you continue to breathe. Feel your body make contact with the seat beneath you. Feel your body resting comfortably, noticing any sensations within your body, without judgment and without wanting anything to change.

4. When you are ready, form an image of yourself in your mind's eye. Picture yourself as you currently sit, and feel your heart open up. Remind yourself that like anyone else, you wish to live happily and in peace. Connect fully with that intention, and feel a sense of warmth and compassion come over you.

5. Continue to hold that image of yourself in your mind's eye. Gently and in silence, repeat the following phrases to yourself:

    • May I be safe.
    • May I be happy.
    • May I be healthy.
    • May I be peaceful and at ease.

6. Take your time, and continue to maintain an image of yourself in your mind's eye. Allow the feelings of peace, tranquility, and compassion to sink in, savoring the meaning of the words. If you notice your mind wandering or drifting, simply observe this and bring your attention back to this moment.

7. When you feel ready, form an image of someone who is easy to feel loving-kindness towards. This could be someone from the past or the present, and can be a friend, family member, loved one, or even a pet. A simple, positive relationship can work best to start with for this practice. Picture that person, and feel your heart open up to them. Remind yourself that like anyone else, you wish for them to live happy and in peace. Connect fully with that intention, and feel a sense of warmth and compassion come over you.

8. As you continue to picture this loved one, gently and in silence repeat the following phrases to yourself:

    • May you be safe.
    • May you be happy.
    • May you be healthy.
    • May you be peaceful and at ease.

Key Points to Consider:

✔ As with any new meditation practice, allow yourself to start slowly. Even a few minutes a day is a great place to start!

✔ As you're getting started, remember to begin by using "simpler," positive relationships as the basis for your practice. Overly complex connections, even with those that we love, can bring up more difficult emotions and make things more challenging as you begin this practice.

How and why it works: The loving-kindness meditation, or *Metta*, holds great promise to increase our well-being in part because it taps into two core ingredients of happiness: connection with others, and kindness. Research shows that when we engage in loving-kindness meditation on an ongoing basis, we begin to relate with others more positively, and these relationships grow closer.

Notes/Impressions:

_____

_____

Seeing the Double Standard

. . . .

Duration: 15-20 minutes

Frequency: Weekly

Level of Difficulty: Moderate

Overview: For many of us, it's far easier to treat others with kindness than it is to treat ourselves in the same way. We can fall into long-standing patterns of self-criticism, in which we constantly beat ourselves up due to feeling as if we don't "measure up" in some way. In fact, some studies suggest that over 80% of people tend to be harder on themselves than they are on others. There are many reasons for this, including internalized messages from childhood, adverse experiences throughout life, as well as ingrained societal beliefs that surround us.

Regardless of the source, recent research underscores how toxic this pattern can be. Rather than motivate us towards something better, self-criticism instead leads us to feel demoralized and disheartened, and takes us further away from our goals. In this exercise, you'll be exploring the differences that you notice between how you tend to treat yourself versus how you treat others, particularly those you care most about.

Instructions: Take a moment and think about a close friend or family member who means a great deal to you. Call this individual to mind, visualizing them, and close your eyes if it helps you to do so. Reflect on who this person is to you, what they've meant to you, and allow yourself to feel how much you care for them. Allow yourself to fully feel the closeness of this connection, and notice the warm and positive feelings that arise. Next, briefly respond to the following questions:

1. *Imagine that this loved one is struggling with a particular issue, and is suffering in a significant way as a result. How might you come to their aid? How would you respond to this person during this time of need? Briefly write down what you might say or do, and the manner in which you would do so.*

_____

_____

_____

2. *Now take a moment and reflect on a time in your life when you were struggling and found yourself suffering in a significant way. How did you respond? How do you tend to react to yourself in these sorts of situations? Briefly write down how you tend to come to your own aid during times of need (or not).*

_____

_____

_____

3. *What differences did you notice when comparing the way you treat yourself to the way you treat others during times of difficulty or suffering? Do you tend to be kinder towards those around you, and if so, what are the ways in which this emerges? What costs, if any, do you think might stem from this pattern? How do you envision your life might be different if you were to learn how to treat yourself with the same degree of compassion that you naturally give others? Write down anything that comes to mind:*

_____

_____

_____

Key Points to Consider:

✔ Don't worry about structure, format, or spelling. Just allow yourself to explore any emotions that arise when tapping into this sense of compassion towards yourself.

✔ Practice when you're calm: In the beginning, many people find it helpful to start practicing this skill when they're feeling more emotionally balanced or calm, rather than when they feel particularly triggered or overwhelmed with difficult emotions.

How and why it works: Many of us fall into patterns of self-criticism in which we're much harder on ourselves than we would ever be towards others. Although we may believe this will help spur us to greater heights, the research is now fairly conclusive that self-criticism is connected to decreased levels of well-being and lower achievement. Conversely, self-compassion has been linked to numerous positive mental and physical health outcomes, including lower rates of depression and anxiety, and higher rates of happiness and well-being.

This exercise helps us to begin this process of learning to be more self-compassionate towards ourselves. By fully noticing and appreciating the ways in which we tend to be harder on ourselves than we are on others, we can begin to notice prime opportunities to cultivate self-compassion.

Notes/Impressions:

_____

_____

_____

_____

_____

_____

_____

_____

Self-Appreciation

. . . .

Duration: 5-10 minutes

Frequency: Weekly or as needed

Level of Difficulty: Moderate

Overview: As many of us know from experience, it's often far easier to focus on our weaknesses than our strengths. This tendency flows from our more common tendency of engaging in self-criticism, which includes magnifying and focusing on our perceived faults at the expense of noticing all that is right with us. Self-compassion teaches us that in order to truly become happy and fulfilled, we must learn to recognize the full picture. This means not only shining a light on our perceived flaws or problems, but also acknowledging and appreciating our positive attributes and accomplishments. Just as we often freely offer praise and encouragement to those around us, we too deserve this same recognition. This exercise helps start this process towards self-appreciation.

Instructions: In the space below, list five things about yourself that you appreciate and feel good about. These can be particular character traits that you view as strengths, accomplishments that you have worked towards, or any other aspect of yourself that you can recognize in a positive light. Remember that if discomfort arises, the aim of this practice isn't to put ourselves up on a pedestal and claim that we're perfect or even better than others; rather, it's to help us learn to appreciate the things we can like about ourselves. *Take a moment to brainstorm, and when you're ready, write them down:*

1. _____

   _____

   _____

2. _____

   _____

   _____

3. _____

_____

_____

4. _____

_____

_____

5. _____

_____

How and why it works: Many of us fall into patterns of self-criticism in which we're much harder on ourselves than we would ever be towards others. Although we may believe this will help spur us to greater heights, the research is now fairly conclusive that self-criticism is connected to decreased levels of well-being and lower achievement levels. Conversely, self-compassion has been linked to numerous positive mental and physical health outcomes, including lower rates of depression and anxiety, and higher rates of happiness and well-being.

One of the many costs associated with self-criticism is that it robs us of the opportunity to truly notice and appreciate our positive aspects. Like anyone else in the world, we are all human beings with strengths and weaknesses, insecurities and frailties, but also gifts and strong points. Part of self-compassion is learning to recognize these more positive elements. This exercise will help you to begin doing this.

Notes/Impressions:

_____

_____

_____

_____

_____

Self-Criticism vs. Self-Compassion

· ·

Duration: 15 minutes

Frequency: Weekly

Level of Difficulty: Moderate

Overview: Although there are many reasons that we sometimes engage in self-criticism, one such reason stems from an internalized belief that self-criticism will somehow spur us on to greater heights and motivate us to improve our shortcomings. Despite how widespread this belief is, research suggests that rather than motivate us, self-criticism instead demoralizes us and makes us less likely to achieve our goals. As an alternative, studies suggest that self-compassion can be an antidote for this tendency, and actually leads to higher levels of achievement and increased motivation. In this exercise, you'll be comparing and contrasting the impact of using either self-criticism or self-compassion when it comes to behavioral change and reaching our goals.

Instructions: Reflect for a moment on a personal trait or habit you tend to be self-critical about, perhaps one which you have tried to change through self-criticism. For example, it could be something about yourself that you don't particularly like, or a bad habit that you've unsuccessfully tried to change.

Habit/trait I struggle with:

_____

_____

_____

Next, take a moment and reflect on how you tend to treat yourself when it comes to this trait or habit. Do you treat yourself with caring, kindness, and understanding? Or do you, like most people, drift into more of a self-critical or self-punitive pattern when it comes to these things? Reflect on how self-criticism impacts you in terms of this issue.

Self-critical language that I use towards myself:

_____

_____

_____

Next, consider the impact of self-criticism in terms of this trait or habit. Does it energize you and help you become a better version of yourself? Or does it instead drag you down and make you feel worse about yourself? Reflect on the toll of self-criticism in regards to this issue.

How self-criticism hurts me:

_____

_____

_____

Once you've completed the previous sections, you've probably noticed that self-criticism tends to make you feel pretty lousy and demoralized. Not only that, it makes us less likely to reach our goals or improve in the ways we'd like to. Assuming that's the case, take a brief moment and consider what it would be like to relate to yourself in a more self-compassionate manner around the particular habit or trait you're struggling with. Rather than beating yourself up, what would it look like if you were to treat yourself the way you'd undoubtedly treat those around you struggling with the same issue?

Self-compassionate alternative:

_____

_____

_____

How and why it works: Many of us fall into patterns of self-criticism, in which we're much harder on ourselves than we would ever be towards others. Although we may believe this will help spur us to greater heights, the research is now fairly conclusive that self-criticism is connected to decreased levels of well-being and lower achievement. Conversely, self-compassion has been linked to numerous positive mental and physical health outcomes, including lower rates of depression and anxiety and higher rates of happiness and well-being.

Notes/Impressions:

_____

_____

_____

_____

_____

_____

_____

_____

CHAPTER 6

Connection

> *Happiness is Love.*
> *Full Stop.*
>
> —George Vaillant

> *We are like islands in the*
> *sea, separate on the surface*
> *but connected in the deep.*
>
> —William James

What Is Connection?

One of the most consistent and robust findings in the field of mental health is that happier people have stronger connections with friends, family, spouses, and co-workers. Moreover, it's not merely a case that happier people tend to have better relationships because they're happy to begin with; rather, there is a clear bidirectional relationship between social connection and well-being.

However, not all connections are created equal, and although we live in a world of infinite connection thanks to technology and social media, the *quality* rather than the *quantity* of our connections is what matters most to our happiness. Not only that, but some research suggests that our *closest* relationships have a disproportionate impact on our happiness. So, for our purposes, we will consider *connection* to mean a sense of closeness and intimacy with the people who matter most to us.

Why Is Connection So Important?

Recent research has shed light on the importance of interpersonal connection as it relates to our happiness and well-being. As it turns out, close interpersonal relationships not only help us feel good; they actually hold the key to a number of psychological, physical, and social benefits as well.

The Psychological Benefits of Connection

Numerous studies now underscore the importance of connection to our psychological well-being and happiness. Indeed, close social support has been linked to significantly lower levels of depression and anxiety, along with reduced stress. In addition, connected individuals have substantially higher rates of happiness and well-being, and are more equipped to bounce back from stress than those with fewer close relationships.

The Health Benefits of Connection

Beyond our mental health and happiness, close interpersonal relationships have been linked to a host of health benefits as well. The most well-supported benefits include stronger immune system functioning, improved sleep quality and quantity, increased longevity, and decreased mortality rates.

The Interpersonal Benefits of Connection

By definition, improving the closeness of our connections enhances our interpersonal relationships. However, it's worth considering some of the vast ways in which social support benefits us: It gives us emotional support when we are struggling, along with tangible and practical support when we are in need. There is even evidence that fostering our interpersonal relationships in the workplace makes us dramatically more likely to get promoted and even earn more money.

The Connected Brain

Many neuroscientists are coming to believe that our brains evolved over time with a key goal in mind: to create and foster close interpersonal relationships. Indeed, there is some evidence that the large size of our prefrontal cortex relative to our body weight is directly linked to our ability to form and maintain social bonds. Additionally, many regions of the brain appear to be involved in interpersonal bonding and relationships.

Beyond the various brain regions associated with interpersonal relationships, a fascinating recent study found that when we experience interpersonal rejection, the same regions of our brains that process physical pain become activated. So, for example, if you were to injure yourself physically in some manner, the same regions would light up as when you experience heartache, or loss. These findings underscore just how crucial social connections are to our lives and to our well-being.

Gratitude Letter and Visit

. . . .

Duration: 30 minutes for writing, plus one hour for the visit

Frequency: Every few months, or more frequently if desired

Level of Difficulty: Moderate/Difficult

Overview: Increasing both gratitude and interpersonal connection are two of the most effective ways to increase our happiness and well-being according to a number of studies. This exercise invites you to cultivate both of these valuable skills, through the direct expression of gratitude towards someone who has helped you in the past. As the name suggests, you'll be writing a letter of thanks to someone important in your life, and delivering your letter directly to that individual.

Instructions: We all have people in our lives—friends, teachers, colleagues, coaches, parents, and so forth—who have helped us a great deal throughout the years. Take a moment and reflect on these individuals, and try to identify one such person who has helped you along the way but whom you haven't fully thanked in the way that you'd like to. For the purposes of this exercise, try to choose someone who lives nearby you, as you will be delivering this letter in the coming days or week. Once you've picked someone, write his or her name.

Person I am grateful towards:

_____

_____

_____

Take a moment, closing your eyes if it's helpful, and reflect on what this person has meant to you, and how they've helped you along the way. Next, write a detailed letter of thanks directed at this individual, keeping the following pieces of guidance in mind. Write down any notes, memories, or reactions that come up for you. After you've done so, use a separate piece of paper (or computer) to write your letter.

- Write your letter directly to this individual.
- Try to be specific—think about particular memories or experiences that are connected to this person.
- Think back on how this individual helped you, and what their presence has meant to you in your life.
- Don't worry too much about spelling or grammar, just be yourself.
- Follow the emotion—try to really feel what this person has meant to you, and allow that sense of gratitude to guide your letter.
- Try to write at least 250-300 words for your gratitude letter.

Dear, _____

_____

_____

_____

_____

_____

_____

_____

_____

_____

_____

_____

_____

Once you've written your letter, arrange to meet this individual (if possible) to deliver your letter in person. Don't tell them the exact purpose of your visit—allow that to be more of a surprise. You might simply tell them that you'd like to meet and have something you'd like to share.

Once you meet this individual face-to-face, let him or her know that you'd like to read a letter of gratitude to them, and that you'd like to share what they mean to you. Take a deep breath and read the letter, trying not to rush through it. As you read, notice whatever emotions come up inside of you, and see if you can notice the other person's emotional reactions as well. Once you're finished, take a moment and share with each other what the experience was like. Before leaving, remember to give the person the letter as a token of your gratitude.

How and why it works: Fostering gratitude and improving our interpersonal relationships are two of the most powerful and effective methods to increasing personal happiness. This practice combines the power of these two factors, by facilitating the expression of gratitude towards someone who's helped you along the way. Studies suggest that the benefits of writing and delivering a "gratitude letter" can be long-lasting, with some research suggesting gains can be maintained for up to two months.

Notes/Impressions:

_____

_____

_____

_____

_____

_____

_____

_____

Unplug and Connect

. . . .

Duration: Flexible

Frequency: Weekly

Level of Difficulty: Easy/Moderate

Overview: In recent years, technology has transformed many parts of our lives, including our interpersonal relationships. Although social media has on the one hand helped facilitate relationships with those around us, several studies have shown that the quality of these relationships has begun to suffer. Indeed, research shows that there is no substitute for genuine, face-to-face, interpersonal connection. This sort of connection nourishes us, and has been shown to have powerful positive effects on our physical and emotional health.

Instructions: We are more connected now than ever. With the tap of a button or the opening of a mobile app, we can reach out to loved ones who may be hundreds or thousands of miles away. But underneath this miraculous change to our world is a somewhat darker truth: The quality of our interpersonal relationships has begun to fray. Indeed, more people report feeling lonely and isolated than at any point in recent history.

Take a moment and reflect on the presence of technology in your life. From your smartphone to your tablet, from your television to your computer, consider the level of interaction you have each and every day with technology in your life. Reflect on how often you find yourself paying attention to your phone or other piece of technology when you are physically with other people. From e-mail, to text messages, to various apps and sports scores, technology has a powerful pull on us, and often draws us away from those we care about most.

For the coming week, choose one interpersonal activity and commit to making it "media free"—no smartphones, no television shows, no texting—just you and the other person. This might mean having a quiet dinner with your spouse, sharing a lunch with a colleague, or going on a hike with a friend. Whatever you choose, commit to sharing that activity fully with the other person.

Once you're done, use the prompts to briefly write down some of your experiences:

- *Activity that I engaged in technology-free:* _____

  _____

  _____

- *Was it easier or more difficult than I expected?* _____

  _____

  _____

- *What was it like emotionally to be fully with the other person?* _____

  _____

  _____

- *Did they seem to notice the difference?* _____

  _____

  _____

- *How was this time different than normal?* _____

  _____

  _____

How and why it works: Fostering our interpersonal relationships is one of the most powerful methods to increasing our happiness according to numerous studies. Although technology and social media has in many ways helped to facilitate our connections with others, the quality of these connections has suffered as a result of some of these changes. This exercise invites you to slow down, unplug, and promote some more genuine and meaningful connections in your life.

Notes/Impressions:

_____

_____

_____

_____

_____

_____

_____

_____

Active-Constructive Responding

· ·

Duration: 10 minutes

Frequency: Daily

Level of Difficulty: Moderate

Overview: In recent years, there has been a significant amount of research done on problematic relationship patterns. For example, we know a great deal about couples who argue constantly, belittle one another, and engage in passive-aggressive behaviors, and the toxic impact that these have on our relationships. However there has been comparatively less research done on *positive* communication patterns, particularly in regard to how we tend to respond to *good* news from those around us.

A psychologist named Shelly Gable wanted to change that, and decided to investigate positive patterns of communication. This next exercise is drawn from her work, and provides you with a powerful tool to help you develop greater closeness and intimacy in your interpersonal relationships. Called **Active-Constructive Responding**, it can be used in your romantic relationships, friendships, or connections at work. As it turns out, how we respond to good news from others has a powerful impact on our interpersonal relationships.

Instructions: According to Gable's research, there are four ways in which we can respond to good news from another person. These four patterns of communication are called:

- **Active-Constructive:** an enthusiastic, engaged, and authentic positive response
- **Passive-Constructive:** a low-energy, disengaged, but somewhat supportive response
- **Active-Destructive:** a dismissive, demeaning, or downplaying response (in other words, "raining on their parade")
- **Passive-Destructive:** a disengaged failure to acknowledge the other person's news

Of these four styles, only active-constructive responding has been shown to improve the quality and closeness of our interpersonal connections. In fact, research suggests that individuals who regularly employ active-constructive responses in their interpersonal relationships have higher levels of happiness and well-being, along with closer connections with others.

What does active-constructive responding look like in real life? Let's say a friend comes to you saying they had just been offered their dream job. According to Gable's research, our four ways of responding would be as follows:

- **Active-Constructive:** "That's amazing news! I'm so proud of you. What do you want to do to celebrate?"
- **Passive-Constructive:** "Oh, that's nice." (Said with little emotion or enthusiasm)
- **Active-Destructive:** "I don't know—isn't that job going to mean a longer commute and tougher hours? Say goodbye to having a life!"
- **Passive-Destructive:** "Hurry up, we're going to be late for our dinner reservation!"

Over the course of the upcoming week, notice the ways in which you respond to others when they share good news with you. Do you tend to respond in an active-constructive manner, which helps amplify and savor their positive success? Or do you tend to drift towards some of the other patterns of communication? Try making a conscious effort to utilize the active-constructive response style in your close interpersonal relationships.

How and why it works: Fostering our interpersonal relationships is one of the most powerful methods to increase our happiness according to numerous studies. Although much research has looked at negative or problematic interpersonal relationship patterns, less attention has been paid to the ingredients of positive interpersonal connection. Active-Constructive Responding is one such ingredient that has been shown to have powerful benefits to our relationships. By actively attending to good news from another person, and helping them feel celebrated and heard, we can foster greater closeness and intimacy with that individual over time.

Notes/Impressions:

_____

_____

_____

_____

_____

_____

_____

The Gratitude "Report Card"

. . . .

Duration: 10 minutes

Frequency: Weekly

Level of Difficulty: Easy/Moderate

Overview: Increasing both gratitude and interpersonal connection are two of the most effective ways to increase our happiness and well-being, according to a number of studies. This exercise invites you to cultivate both of these valuable skills, through the direct expression of gratitude towards someone who you see on a regular basis, but whom you would like to thank in a more genuine or thoughtful manner.

Just as it can be easier to focus on the stressful parts of our lives, or the areas that we're unhappy about, it can similarly be easier to focus on what's wrong in our relationships rather than what's right. Whether in our romantic relationships or our friendships, we all fall prone from time to time to focus on our frustrations while taking the positive aspects more for granted. This next exercise helps you to counteract this negativity bias in our interpersonal relationships, and is called the Gratitude "Report Card."

Instructions: Over the next week, choose one person in your life with whom you have a close relationship. Ideally, this will be someone who you see on a regular basis, whether at home, work, or school. It could be a romantic partner, a close friend, a family member, or a colleague.

Each day, write down at least one thing that you appreciate about that person, or one thing they did or said for which you are thankful. These sources of gratitude can range in size or scope, but the important thing is that you identify at least one thing each day to write down. At the end of the week, have a face-to-face conversation with this individual to express your thanks to them. Share your list with them, and express how much they mean to you and how much you appreciate them.

Person I am grateful for: _____

Gratitude list:

Day 1: _____

_____

_____

Day 2: _____

_____

_____

Day 3: _____

_____

_____

Day 4: _____

_____

_____

Day 5: _____

_____

_____

Day 6: _____

_____

_____

Day 7: _____

_____

_____

How and why it works: The Gratitude "Report Card" can be a powerful exercise for a number of reasons. First, it helps us to foster two key ingredients for happiness and well-being: gratitude and close interpersonal connections. In addition, it helps us to combat our brain's natural negativity bias, which leads us to often focus on what's wrong rather than what's right in our lives.

Notes/Impressions:

_____

_____

_____

_____

_____

_____

_____

_____

Listen Actively

· · · · · · · · · · · · · · · · · ·

Duration: 15 minutes

Frequency: Flexible

Level of Difficulty: Moderate/Difficult

Overview: Whether due to exhaustion or feeling stretched thin, many of us often shortchange our face-to-face interactions and aren't fully present when interacting with those we care about. In essence, we find ourselves listening to another person without *really* hearing what they have to say. As a result, we miss out on genuine opportunities for connection, and may even leave that person feeling a bit hurt or rejected.

In this practice, you'll be communicating with another person in your life in a more active and engaged manner—a technique called "Active Listening." This skill can be used with a spouse, a coworker, a friend, or anyone else you'd like to connect with more.

Instructions: Over the course of the coming week, identify one person in your life who you'd like to connect with on a more genuine level. When you interact with that individual, try keeping the following five communication habits in mind as you're conversing with them:

- **Summarize and paraphrase:** Once the other person finishes speaking, try paraphrasing back what he or she said to ensure that you fully understood, and to demonstrate that you were *really* listening. You might try starting off your statements with phrases such as "It sounds like you're saying," or "If I'm hearing you right," and so forth.

- **Empathize:** If the other person has expressed something difficult, or seems to be struggling, try putting yourself in their shoes and conveying to them that you care. You might try phrases such as "That sounds really difficult," or "I can see how that would be really painful."

- **Be mindful of body language and tone:** Much of communication is nonverbal, and things like our posture, tone, and body language can make a big difference when we're trying to communicate effectively. Try to make solid eye contact, and keep an open posture. Try to avoid facial expressions that demonstrate frustration or irritation.

- **Ask questions:** One of the best ways to help the other person feel comfortable and secure around us is to ask encouraging, thoughtful questions, inviting them to share more. This conveys respect and interest in what they have to say, and can also help clarify anything that we're unsure of or unclear on.

- **Cut down on advice-giving:** When we're focusing on listening, a key thing to remember is to avoid jumping in with advice or problem-solving. This can make the other person feel shut down, and conveys that you're more interested in fixing the situation than hearing them out.

How and why it works: When we listen actively, we help others in our life feel understood and heard, and we help foster closer relationships with these individuals. By using the five micro-skills of active listening outlined above, we convey respect and caring to the people in our lives, and help them feel more able to share further with us.

Notes/Impressions:

_____

_____

_____

_____

_____

_____

_____

CHAPTER 7

Optimism

> *Men are disturbed not by things, but by what we make of them.*
>
> —Epictetus

> *Our life is a creation of our mind.*
>
> —The Buddha

What Is Optimism?

The concept of optimism may mean different things to different people, and therefore requires a bit of unpacking. The word optimism itself comes from the Latin word *optimum*, which roughly translates to mean "best." At its core, to be optimistic is closely connected with the ability to see things in a good light, both in terms of our future as well as events that are occuring in our lives. The key type of optimism that we will be practicing in this book is referred to as *dispositional optimism*, and is defined as follows:

- Having hope or confidence regarding the future
- Believing that challenges and obstacles can be overcome

In other words, when we reflect on our future, do we look forward to it with anticipation, expecting that things will turn out well? Or do we nervously glance ahead with worry, believing that storm clouds are approaching? Generally speaking, optimists believe that the coming days will be positive, and that they will be able to accomplish many of their hopes and dreams. Optimism does not mean that life is without challenge or pain, and in fact a key component of optimism is to be able to see things in a realistic (rather than overly pessimistic) light.

Why Practice Optimism?

We are often told to "look on the bright side" or learn to "see the glass as half full." Although these sorts of recommendations seem trivial, they nonetheless hold great truth. In short, there have now been countless studies showing both the negative consequences associated with pessimism, as well as the numerous benefits linked to optimism. By training ourselves to become more optimistic, we can reap a wide range of benefits for our mental health and physical well-being.

The Psychological Benefits of Optimism

Whereas pessimism has been closely linked to a number of negative outcomes including depression, anxiety, and even suicide, optimism has been found to be among the most important ingredients for a life of happiness and well-being. Studies show that individuals who are more optimistic have lower rates of depression and anxiety, higher rates of life satisfaction and happiness, and are more resilient in the face of stress. It is thought that one of the key benefits of optimism is that it short-circuits rumination, which is strongly linked to negative mood states like depression and anxiety.

The Health Benefits of Optimism

Not only are grateful individuals happier, research suggests that they are healthier as well. Studies have found that individuals who regularly practice gratitude have improved overall physical health, stronger immune systems, and reduced rates of stress-related illnesses. Not only that, but research has linked the practice of gratitude to other benefits such as getting better sleep (as much as an extra hour per night), and exercising more (as much as 90 minutes more per week).

The Interpersonal Benefits of Optimism

Grateful individuals have stronger interpersonal relationships, including more satisfying romantic relationships, across a number of studies. They also are more altruistic and likely to donate to charities and engage in volunteer work, and are even more able to let go of resentments and foster forgiveness.

The Optimistic Brain

Cultivating optimism impacts our brain in a number of ways according to the latest research. First, optimists tend to display greater activation in their left prefrontal cortex, an area of the brain closely linked to positive emotional states. Additionally, they show decreased sensitivity in their amygdala, the small part of our brain that fires up our fight-or-flight response during times of stress. Finally, optimists display greater activation in a region of the brain known as the orbitofrontal cortex, which is associated with helping us to better regulate our emotions and decrease our anxiety.

Slow and Steady Wins the Race

· ·

Duration: 10 minutes

Frequency: As needed

Level of Difficulty: Easy

Overview: Pessimism often stems from feeling that we cannot possibly reach the finish line from where we are standing. We look off in the distance and see our goals, but the ground in between where we are standing and where we wish to go can feel insurmountable. But just as we cannot scale an entire ladder in one single step, we must remember that the path for reaching our goals can be a longer journey.

The Chinese philosopher Lao Tzu famously stated that the "journey of a thousand miles begins with a single step." When it comes to fostering hope towards the future and moving towards meaningful goals, it can help to keep this spirit in mind. In this optimism-building exercise, you'll be identifying important goals that you have for the future, and breaking them up into more manageable sub-goals. Whereas the larger goals can sometimes feel unattainable (like viewing the summit of a mountain when you're just about to climb it), the steps in between can often feel much more manageable. By focusing on these instead, we can begin shifting from a place of pessimism to a more optimistic mindset.

Instructions: Take a moment and reflect on some of the goals and dreams you have for the future. Consider various domains of your life, including your professional life, relationships, friendships, family, and hobbies. Although reflecting on these goals can feel exciting, it can also bring about feelings of dread or pessimism particularly if they feel rather far off. To overcome this obstacle, it helps to break down our larger goals into shorter sub-goals that can be completed one small step at a time. Feel free to use the prompting questions to help get you started:

A long-term goal I have:

_____

_____

_____

When I hope to achieve this by:

_____

_____

_____

What is the first step I need to take in order to achieve this goal?

_____

_____

_____

Who can I turn to for support in helping me reach this goal?

_____

_____

_____

If I made progress towards this in the coming weeks, what would that look like?

_____

_____

_____

If I made progress in the coming months, what would that look like?

_____

_____

_____

In the process of setting sub-goals, it can help to keep in mind the concept of "SMART Goals." SMART Goals are:

- **S**pecific—the goal is clearly defined (e.g., who, what, where, when, and why)
- **M**easurable—the goal can be tracked in terms of progress (e.g., how much, how many)
- **A**chievable—the goal is attainable and realistic
- **R**elevant—the goal is worthwhile and related to our larger goals and dreams
- **T**imely—the goal has a time limit (e.g., when will it be accomplished by?)

By combining the focus questions contained above with the parameters of SMART Goals, you'll be well on your way to moving toward your goals!

Notes/Impressions:

_____

_____

_____

_____

_____

_____

_____

_____

Overcoming Pessimism

. . . .

Duration: 15 minutes

Frequency: As needed

Level of Difficulty: Easy/Moderate

Overview: We all engage in negative thinking from time to time. But negative, pessimistic self-talk that persists can come at a great cost. It can demoralize us, lower our mood, and make us less likely to pursue and achieve our goals. Even worse, pessimistic thinking can create a downward spiral, in which negative thoughts create negative mood states, which in turn produce further feelings of pessimism. Although this pattern can occur unconsciously and automatically, we can through mindfulness and awareness learn to notice these patterns occurring and stop them in their tracks.

In this optimism-boosting exercise, you'll first learn to notice and identify the negative and pessimistic thoughts that get in your way. In the next step, you'll practice replacing them with a more realistic way of thinking. As the Greek philosopher Epictetus pointed out, we are "disturbed not by things, but by what we make of them." In other words, our mindset has a powerful impact on our emotional experience and our behaviors. By slowly learning how to shift our thinking away from pessimism and negativity and more towards optimism, we can change the way we feel by changing the way that we think.

Instructions: Over the course of the next week, notice and write down some of the negative or pessimistic thoughts that get in the way of your happiness. Monitor your inner self-talk for the sorts of thoughts that are most problematic for you. For example, when you feel discouraged or frustrated, you might notice thoughts running through your mind such as "I'm such a failure," or "I'll never be able to finish this project." Whenever you feel bad in a given moment, bring your awareness to the way in which you are internally "talking" to yourself, for this self-talk has a powerful impact on the way we feel. Once you've noticed some of these negative beliefs or thoughts, write them down.

Negative Thought #1:

_____

_____

_____

Negative Thought #2:

_____

_____

_____

Negative Thought #3:

_____

_____

_____

Negative Thought #4:

_____

_____

_____

Negative Thought #5:

_____

_____

_____

Next, begin the process of challenging these negative thoughts and beliefs. See if you can reinterpret the situation in a more realistic and optimistic manner. Remember to strive for balanced, positive thoughts. To help you in this process, feel free to use the following format to help facilitate these changes:

- Negative thought I am trying to change: _____
- What would I say to a close friend or a loved one in this situation?

- What might a close friend or loved one say to me?
- Is this thought a fact? Or is it merely a thought? If I choose to view it as just a thought, does that change how it affects me?
- Is there another way to look at this situation?
- Are there any factors I may be missing here?
- How important is this in the grand scheme of things?
- Am I overgeneralizing, or missing the bigger picture here?
- What would be a more balanced or neutral way of looking at this situation?

How and why it works: Although we all struggle from time to time with negative self-talk or doubt, chronic pessimism has been linked to a host of adverse outcomes when it comes to our mental and physical health. To become a more optimistic person, one of the best places to start is by shifting our mindset away from the negative and more towards the positive. By learning to view our lives in a realistically-positive manner, we become more likely to achieve our goals and are able to enhance our well-being.

Notes/Impressions:

_____

_____

_____

_____

_____

_____

_____

_____

A Positive Future

. . . .

Duration: 15 minutes

Frequency: Daily for one week

Level of Difficulty: Moderate

Overview: When it comes to developing an optimistic mindset, one of the most powerful ways to do so is to cultivate a positive view of the future. This exercise is drawn from the work of psychologist Laura King, and is designed to help us do exactly that. In King's study, she invited participants to engage in roughly 20 minutes of journal writing over the course of several days, with a particular focus in mind. Specifically, participants were asked to imagine their "best possible future self," and to write about their future if all their hopes and dreams were to come true.

Although it might not seem that such a brief writing exercise would yield such powerful results, the findings from King's studies were remarkable. Compared to those in a control group, individuals who wrote about their "best possible future" were found to be significantly happier even weeks later. Not only that, but they had better physical health outcomes and were less likely to fall ill, with these gains lasting for several months.

Why did this simple exercise yield such powerful changes? It appears that not only did the writing exercise help individuals feel better in the moment; it also helped them feel empowered to begin making tangible and concrete positive changes in their lives. Writing about their "best possible future self" may have also helped the participants tap into and identify what they valued most in life, and inspired them to set goals to help them live in a more aligned way with these values.

Instructions: For the next week, set aside 20 minutes per day to journal about your life in the future. For this practice, try imagining that in this future, various aspects of your life have begun to really fall into place. What is the best possible future that you can imagine?

Picture yourself 5 or 10 years from now, or even further into the future if you'd like—consider the various domains of your life, including your relationships, your work, your health, and your hobbies. Close your eyes if it helps, and picture what your life would look like if your dreams became realized and you achieved your most meaningful goals.

Spend the next 20 minutes free-writing about this best possible future. Feel free to use the space below to get the ball rolling. And keep in mind the following guidelines if they help you in the process:

- Don't worry about spelling or grammar—just write whatever comes up for you as you envision the future in this way.
- Don't worry if the positive future seems far off, or unrealistic in any way. Just try to envision your best self, and what your life would look like if your dreams came true.
- Try to be specific—instead of envisioning vague possibilities, see if you can hash them out a bit more and be a bit more concrete.
- Experiment a bit—try focusing on different time-points (e.g., a year from now, five years from now, 10 years from now, and so forth), as well as different parts of your life (e.g., your romantic relationship, your friendships, your professional life, family, and so forth).

_____

_____

_____

_____

_____

How and why it works: This practice helps us become more optimistic and achieve greater levels of happiness in a number of ways. First, it helps us to get in touch with our core values—the parts of our lives we hold most dear—and gives us ideas of how we might live more according to these values. Second, this practice helps boost optimism by creating a sense of hopefulness towards the future. Third, this particular practice can help us see that these dreams are within our grasp. As a result, we can begin taking even small steps towards them in the coming days.

Notes/Impressions:

_____

_____

_____

_____

Reflecting on Success

. . . .

Duration: 15 minutes

Frequency: As needed

Level of Difficulty: Moderate

Overview: One of the best ways to remind ourselves that the future will turn out well is to look in a somewhat unlikely place—the past! Indeed, by reflecting on times in which we have already overcome some obstacle or gotten through a time of difficulty, we can build optimism towards our current circumstances and the future. In this exercise, you'll be reflecting on times from the past in which you had success, or in which you overcame an obstacle, in order to learn from these experiences moving forward.

Instructions: Take a moment and reflect on a time from the past in which you were able to achieve an important goal. Consider various areas of your life, such as your relationships, your job, or your success in school. *Choose one of those successes and write about it:*

_____

_____

_____

_____

_____

Next, use the following questions as prompts to help you reflect on this success, and to learn from it:

- How hard did you have to work to attain this goal?
- What aspects of your character, or personal strengths, did you tap into in reaching this goal?
- Were there times when you thought of giving up in your pursuit of this goal? If so, what enabled you to keep going?
- Who did you receive support from during that time period? Who cheered you on during your successes?
- What did you learn about yourself in attaining this goal?
- How does it feel emotionally to reflect on this time of success?
- What can you take from this past experience and apply to your life now?

How and why it works: When times get tough, it's easy for that pessimistic inner voice to creep in. Rather than give in to this, one of the best methods for boosting our sense of hope and optimism is to reflect back on times when we've achieved an important goal, or overcome a difficult obstacle. In doing so, we are able to see the strength that exists within us, and tap into it as we face the future.

Notes/Impressions:

_____

_____

_____

_____

_____

_____

_____

_____

_____

Finding the Silver Linings

. . . .

Duration: 15 minutes

Frequency: Weekly

Level of Difficulty: Easy

Overview: It's natural to find yourself ruminating on things that have gone wrong in life, and to fixate on the negative. Our brain's negativity bias makes it such that our minds naturally gravitate and get stuck on negative events far more than positive ones. However, the ability to "look on the bright side" or to train our minds to "view the glass as half full" is a key element of optimism.

This practice is designed to help you reinterpret challenges and setbacks through the lens of optimism. Rather than viewing setbacks as overwhelming obstacles that we cannot overcome, optimism allows us to view these challenges as conquerable and achievable. Research suggests that training ourselves to see the bright side even during difficult times is a core component of optimism and a key element of well-being. This practice helps you to find the silver lining following setbacks.

Instructions: First, try to call to mind a time in your life when you overcame an obstacle or were able to achieve something in spite of a difficult challenge. *Take a moment and identify one such instance, really getting in touch with it on an emotional level, and write about it:*

_____

_____

_____

_____

_____

Once you have completed the above step, Shift your focus now to a recent time in which something didn't go well. Perhaps it was a recent situation at work, or a difficult interaction at home. *After you've identified one such situation, write it down:*

_____

_____

_____

_____

_____

Next, see if you can reframe this difficult or stressful situation in a new light. Try to see if you can find the silver lining, or gain a new perspective on it. Some helpful questions might include:

- How important will this feel a year from now? Five years from now? 10 years?
- Did anything good come of this difficult situation?
- Which parts of how I handled it can I feel proud of?
- What can I learn from what happened?

With those in mind, take a few moments and write down how you might find the bright side of this situation:

_____

_____

_____

_____

_____

How and why it works: Optimists perform better than pessimists across a range of areas, including psychological well-being, physical health, job performance, and more. A key thing that differentiates optimists from pessimists is how they respond in the face of adversity. Whereas pessimists tend to be demoralized by challenges, optimists are able to see the silver linings and engage in healthy problem-solving around difficult situations. This practice helps to tap into this very component of optimism, and helps you to reframe a recent challenge in a more positive light.

Notes/Impressions:

_____

_____

_____

_____

_____

_____

_____

_____

CHAPTER 8

Forgiveness

> *Resentment is like drinking poison and then hoping it will kill your enemies.*
>
> —Nelson Mandela

> *To err is human; to forgive, divine.*
>
> —Alexander Pope

What Is Forgiveness?

Forgiveness is a complicated topic, and there are many misconceptions about what it means to forgive. For our purposes, and to have common language and understanding around the topic, we will consider forgiveness to be defined as:

- A conscious effort to let go of anger and resentment towards a person or group who has harmed us; and
- Liberating ourselves from motivations for revenge and being able to feel peace in the present moment in spite of what may have happened in the past.

A key aspect of forgiveness is remembering that it is for you, and you alone. It means choosing to let go of resentment or bitterness you've been holding onto in order to allow yourself to find happiness and peace. Further, it means taking back the power we've given away by holding onto resentment, and prioritizing our own healing and well-being. Just as it's important to define what forgiveness is, it's also imperative to remind ourselves of what forgiveness is *not*. Forgiveness is not:

- *Forgetting*—we can and should remember what has happened, in order to shape our choices and behaviors moving forward.
- *Condoning or minimizing*—when we forgive, we are not condoning what has happened; rather, we are choosing to no longer give away space in our minds and hearts "rent-free."
- *Reconciling*—although we may choose to reconcile with the person who hurt us, we may at other times choose to no longer associate with the other person while still effectively forgiving them.

Why Practice Forgiveness?

Painful experiences are an inevitable part of life. But when we hold onto those painful experiences for months or even years, it turns into resentment. Over time, resentment and bitterness is hazardous to our health. Research underscores the toll that resentment and chronic anger take on our minds, bodies, and relationships. On the other hand, letting go of a grudge and choosing forgiveness, has tremendous implications for our happiness and for our health.

The Psychological Benefits of Forgiveness

In contrast to resentment, forgiveness is associated with a host of mental health benefits. Individuals who are able to forgive have significantly higher levels of well-being and happiness, and have lower rates of depression, anxiety, and stress. In the face of stressors, forgiving individuals are far more resilient and bounce back more quickly during challenging times.

The Health Benefits of Forgiveness

When we hold onto resentment and anger, it takes an immense toll on our bodies: Stress hormones are chronically released through the body, and there are adverse outcomes that include a weakened immune system, heart disease, high blood pressure, and chronic illness. In the short-term, choosing to forgive can help relieve the unpleasant feelings of anger that we experience when we're hurt. But more importantly, in the long-run it can help reverse many of the negative outcomes listed above.

The Interpersonal Benefits of Forgiveness

When we hold onto a grudge, our relationships suffer, and not merely with the person we're angry at. Instead, anger and resentment tend to bleed into other areas of our lives. So even if one chooses to forgive without reconciling with the person who hurt them, studies show that their other relationships will improve as a result of this choice. Beyond that, research has shown that forgiving individuals are actually more altruistic, and tend to donate more time and money to causes they believe in.

The Forgiving Brain

The practice of forgiveness impacts the brain in a number of ways, according to recent research. First, brain scans reveal that when a person forgives they experience decreased activation in their amygdala, a small region of the brain associated with activating our fight-or-flight response. In addition, research shows that individuals who forgive experience increased activation in two specific regions of the brain: the inferior parietal cortex and the precuneus. These two areas are associated with things like empathy and the ability to see things from another person's perspective. Considering that forgiveness oftentimes flows from being able to see the other person as human, these findings make intuitive sense.

Cost-Benefit Analysis of Forgiveness

· ·

Duration: 10 minutes

Frequency: As needed

Level of Difficulty: Moderate

Overview: When we've been wronged, anger is a natural and human emotional experience, and there is nothing wrong with feeling anger (certain behaviors associated with anger may, however, be a different story). But holding onto anger, and chronically feeling resentful, can cause us a considerable amount of suffering. Indeed, long-term resentment has been associated with increased levels of stress, diminished mental health, and physical health problems.

The antidote for this, of course, is to choose to forgive and let go. Forgiveness can help undo the psychological and physiological effects of holding a grudge, and can help us take back the power in our own lives. But before choosing to forgive another person, it's important to fully weigh the implications of this choice. There are indeed many reasons we might have for not wanting to forgive another person, and rushing into a decision to forgive can have negative consequences as well.

In order to explore this more fully, it can help to pause and reflect on both the pros and cons of forgiveness. In this practice, you'll be weighing the costs and benefits of choosing to forgive.

Instructions: Reflect for a moment on people in your life who have hurt you in some way, and who you have not yet forgiven. *Choose one such instance, and write about it:*

Person who hurt me: _____

What that person did to me: _____

_____

_____

Take a moment now and reflect on how the person's behavior has impacted your life. Consider how their actions hurt you emotionally, physically, or otherwise. Allow yourself to get in touch with these feelings, difficult as they may be. *Write down the ways in which this individual hurt you:*

_____

_____

_____

How their actions harmed me:

_____

_____

_____

Next, consider the ways in which holding onto your resentment has affected your health, your relationships with other people, and so forth over the years. Take a moment and reflect on this, and write down any observations you come up with.

Ways in which resentment has hurt me:

_____

_____

_____

With that in mind, consider the costs and benefits of choosing to forgive this individual. For example, on the one hand you may feel as if he or she doesn't deserve your forgiveness; on the other hand, you may realize that holding onto this anger for any longer will continue to hurt only you. *Reflect on the various pros and cons of your choice to forgive, and write down anything that comes to mind.*

Benefits of Choosing Forgiveness	Costs of Choosing Forgiveness

Once you have completed the previous table, take a moment and reflect on what you discovered. Use the following questions to explore your experience more fully:

- Was there anything surprising about what I found?
- Was either side (benefits or costs) more powerful or persuasive?
- How do I think my life would change if I were to forgive this person?
- Did exploring the pros and cons of forgiveness move me in either direction?

How and why it works: Rushing into a decision to forgive can have several adverse consequences, including increasing our feelings of resentment as well as a likelihood that our decision will not "stick." As a result, it's important to first and foremost explore whether we even truly want to forgive the other person. This practice helps us to determine whether we do, in fact, want to move towards a decision to forgive.

Notes/Impressions:

_____

_____

_____

_____

_____

_____

A Letter of Forgiveness

. . . .

Duration: 20 minutes

Frequency: As needed

Level of Difficulty: Moderate/Difficult

Overview: When we've been wronged, anger is a natural and human emotional experience, and there is nothing wrong with feeling anger (certain behaviors associated with anger may, however, be a different story). But holding onto anger, and chronically feeling resentful, can cause us a considerable amount of suffering. Indeed, long-term resentment has been associated with increased levels of stress, diminished mental health, and physical health problems.

The antidote for this, of course, is to choose to forgive and let go. Forgiveness can help undo the psychological and physiological effects of holding a grudge, and can help us take back the power in our own lives. By choosing to forgive, we are able to let go of the pain we've been holding onto, and return to a life of happiness, tranquility, and peace. It's important to remember that forgiveness is *not* about the other person; rather, it's for you, and you alone. Remember too that forgiveness does not mean condoning, forgetting, or agreeing with the other person's behaviors and choices. Instead, true forgiveness involves making a choice that you are no longer willing to allow what happened in the past to ruin your future.

In this exercise, you'll be writing a letter of forgiveness. Studies show that doing so can help us to fully process our feelings related to what happened, and to begin experiencing the benefits associated with forgiveness.

Instructions: Reflect for a moment on people in your life who have hurt you in some way, and who you have not yet forgiven. *Choose one such instance, and write about it:*

Person who hurt me: _____

What that person did to me:

_____

_____

_____

Next, consider the ways in which holding onto your resentment has affected you over the years. Reflect on various domains of your life, such as your health, your relationships with other people, and so forth. *Take a moment and reflect on this, and write down any observations you come up with.*

Ways in which resentment has hurt me:

_____

_____

_____

_____

_____

_____

Next, write a detailed letter of forgiveness to this individual on a separate piece of paper or on the next page. In this letter, explain the way in which you felt hurt by this person's actions towards you, and how you have continued to suffer as a result. Finally, end the letter with an expression of forgiveness towards that person. Let them know that you are choosing to let go of your anger and move on with your life. Remember, you do *not* have to send this letter; this is a step you are taking for you.

Feel free to consider the following questions to help you get started in writing your letter:

- What did this person mean to me?
- How has holding onto the resentment hurt me?
- Has my anger towards this person held me back from my own happiness and peace?
- How long ago did the offense occur? Was it recent or further back in the past?
- How has my anger towards this person impacted my life? How has it impacted their life?
- What would it be like to live free from these feelings of resentment?

Once you have reflected on these questions, begin writing your letter here or on a separate sheet of paper:

Dear, _____

_____

_____

_____

_____

_____

_____

_____

_____

_____

_____

_____

_____

_____

_____

How and why it works: Expressive writing has been shown to be helpful for a number of issues, including forgiveness. In writing this letter of forgiveness, you'll be able to explore the emotional impact of the other person's action, process the feelings that you've been holding onto, and weigh whether or not forgiving the other person feels like the right choice for you at this point in time.

Notes/Impressions:

_____

_____

_____

_____

_____

_____

_____

_____

Recalling Forgiveness

· ·

Duration: 15 minutes

Frequency: As needed

Level of Difficulty: Moderate

Overview: Choosing to forgive can be one of the most challenging decisions we can make. There are indeed many barriers to forgiveness, including misconceptions about what it means to forgive, as well as not having properly grieved before preparing to forgive. If you find yourself feeling stuck and struggling to move towards a place of forgiveness, it can often be helpful to reflect on instances in which we have been on the receiving end of forgiveness—by doing so, we can begin breaking down our own barriers to forgiveness, and also gain a greater understanding and appreciation of the benefits of forgiveness.

Instructions: Take a moment and reflect on a time in which you hurt someone you cared about, whether intentionally or accidentally. Perhaps you said something harsh to a loved one, or maybe it was a time when you acted insensitively towards a friend. *Call to mind one of these situations, and write about it:*

_____

_____

_____

_____

_____

_____

Next, reflect on the other person's decision to forgive you. Consider what it was like for you to be on the receiving end of their forgiveness, and how their decision to forgive you impacted your life moving forward. Close your eyes if it helps, and really take a moment to fully explore this experience of receiving forgiveness. *When you're ready, use the questions to explore this experience more fully.*

Person who forgave me:

_____

_____

_____

How did they convey their forgiveness to me?

_____

_____

_____

How did their forgiveness affect me?

_____

_____

_____

How might their decision to forgive have affected them?

_____

_____

_____

Did my relationship with this person change following their decision to forgive me? If so, how?

_____

_____

_____

What can I learn from their decision to forgive me?

_____

_____

_____

How and why it works: Research shows that one of the most effective ways we can move towards a decision to forgive can occur when we reflect on times when we've been on the receiving end of forgiveness. This practice helps us to get in touch with the feelings we've experienced from being forgiven, which can help facilitate our own movement towards letting go of resentments.

Notes/Impressions:

_____

_____

_____

_____

_____

_____

_____

_____

Forgiveness Meditation

· ·

Duration: 15 minutes

Frequency: As needed

Level of Difficulty: Easy

Overview: Choosing to forgive can be one of the most challenging decisions we can make. There are indeed many barriers to forgiveness, including misconceptions about what it means to forgive, as well as not having properly grieved before preparing to forgive. If you find yourself feeling stuck and struggling to move towards a place of forgiveness, one powerful way to begin facilitating this process is to practice a forgiveness meditation.

For some people, this exercise can initially bring about some painful experiences associated with the hurt they've encountered. Yet for many, it can be a valuable experiential exercise that can help promote healing and recovery. For the purposes of this meditation, choose someone in your life towards whom you continue to harbor anger, resentment, or hostility. When first starting out, try choosing a relatively minor offense (rather than your deepest source of pain), and then work your way up from there. Once you've identified an individual to focus on during this practice, use the instructions to guide you in your meditation.

Instructions: Begin by finding a comfortable, peaceful place to sit. Sit in a manner that's comfortable for you, either in a chair or on the ground. Keep your back straight, allowing your shoulders to relax. Close your eyes, or if it feels more comfortable, focus your gaze softly on the ground in front of you.

Begin by taking three easy and gentle breaths, followed by slow and steady exhales. With each breath, feel yourself slowing down and becoming more immersed in the present moment.

If you notice your mind wandering or your thoughts drifting during this exercise, simply notice this and return your attention and awareness each time to your breath. You may notice your mind drifting off or wandering at many points during this meditation, and that's totally okay. That's simply the mind doing what it does. Observe this tendency, and without judgment, return your awareness to the present moment.

Bring your awareness now to your breathing. Notice the sensation of your breath entering and leaving your body. With each breath, observe yourself becoming more present in the moment. Let your mind and body relax and settle into this moment.

When you are ready, allow yourself to visualize the person who has hurt you. As you do, allow yourself to feel the emotions you've been carrying with you as a result of not forgiving them. Continuing to breathe, reflect on the feelings of resentment, or even anger, that you've been holding onto. Feel these feelings in your body.

Notice what happens in your mind and in your body when you think of this person and the pain they have caused you. You may notice difficult memories coming up, and you might even notice some physiological changes in your body, such as increased heart rate or muscle tension. Strong emotions may start to well up, and that's okay too. Allow yourself to feel whatever feelings arise. Remind yourself that the pain you feel now is a result of both what happened in the past, and continually carrying this burden.

When you feel ready, allow your heart to begin opening up as you prepare to offer forgiveness to this person who hurt you. Say the following phrases out loud:

"You have caused me hurt and pain, but I have carried this burden for too long. To the extent that I am ready and able, I offer you forgiveness. You have caused me harm, and you have hurt me. But I choose to forgive you."

As you continue to breathe, repeat the following words:

"I forgive you."

"I forgive you."

"I forgive you."

Begin to feel your heart open up further, and notice the weight starting to lift off of you. Slowly feel the painful emotions melt away, and notice a feeling of calmness starting to wash over you.

As you continue to breathe, feel the burden of bitterness soften, and allow yourself to feel a sense of tranquility come over you. For the next minute, simply sit and breathe, allowing these feelings to fully sink in. When you are ready, slowly open your eyes.

How and why it works: This meditation can be a powerful experiential practice that allows us to emotionally process the experience of forgiveness. By meditating on the choice to forgive, we can begin to emotionally prepare ourselves to let go of our pain and resentment, and to choose freedom from these burdens.

Notes/Impressions:

_____

_____

_____

_____

_____

_____

_____

_____

Drawing Strength from Adversity

· ·

Duration: 15 minutes

Frequency: As needed

Level of Difficulty: Moderate

Overview: As many of us know, it can be all too easy to find ourselves stuck in a downward spiral after someone close to us causes us pain. Whether we are hurt by a cruel comment from our boss, infidelity in our relationship, or pain inflicted on us by family members, we can find ourselves stuck in these feelings of anger and resentment. Worse yet, these feelings can often fester, causing us distress many months or even years after the incident occurred.

Although it may seem counterintuitive at first, much research suggests that an important part of the healing process is learning to shift our focus away from the grievance version of our story and more towards one of strength and resiliency. As an alternative to feeling stuck in a narrative of being damaged or hurt, we can instead choose to focus on the *positive* things that resulted from this difficult experience. Remember, this doesn't mean that what happened was positive; rather, it means that oftentimes something positive resulted from it nonetheless (such as learning who our true friends are, or learning to value ourselves in a different manner).

Even when we experience something painful or traumatic, some studies suggest that learning to identify the benefits that we gained from this adverse experience can help us see ourselves in a new light. Over time, this shift in focus can help lay the groundwork for us to let go of our anger and resentment, and to be able to forgive more fully.

Instructions: Find a quiet place to sit and reflect. Begin by thinking about a person who has harmed you in some way in the past, whether physically or emotionally. The incident should be from the past, and not an ongoing offense. Reflect on what the person did to you, how they hurt you, and how your life was impacted following the incident. *Once you've identified one such situation, write about what happened:*

_____

_____

_____

_____

_____

_____

Next, spend about 15 minutes writing only about the positive things that occurred as a result of this difficult experience. This might feel difficult initially, but take your time and consider various aspects of your life. Consider the ways in which you've grown as a result of what happened, how you have changed (perhaps for the better) as a result of the experience, and how you've become stronger from it. Consider these questions in your reflection.

1. *Have you grown in some way as a result of what happened?*

_____

_____

_____

2. *Have you learned anything about yourself because of this incident?*

_____

_____

_____

3. *Have you grown closer with anyone in your life because of what occurred?*

_____

_____

_____

4. *Did you learn whom you could turn to and trust during a time of need?*

_____

_____

_____

5. *Do you have a greater sense of personal value since the incident?*

_____

_____

_____

6. *Do you have a clearer sense of your own needs and values since this happened?*

_____

_____

_____

7. *Are you able to appreciate anything more in life since the incident?*

_____

_____

_____

8. *Have you grown to be more self-reliant?*

_____

_____

_____

9. *Do you feel that you've become more empathetic and compassionate towards others as a result of your own difficult experiences?*

_____

_____

_____

How and why it works: When we've been hurt by another person, many of us fall into a pattern of blame and resentment. We focus on the source of our hurt, and the ways in which our lives have been negatively impacted by the other person's actions. However, following many difficult situations in life, including when we've been hurt by another person, there are opportunities for growth.

Notes/Impressions:

_____

_____

_____

_____

_____

_____

_____

Empathize

. . . .

Duration: 15 minutes

Frequency: As needed

Level of Difficulty: Moderate

Overview: Experiencing hurt at the hands of someone we care about is an inevitable part of life. We've all been treated poorly, experienced rejection, or had our hearts broken. The pain we feel in these moments is normal, and entirely human. But all too often, the pain lingers and remains with us for weeks, months, or even years, causing us further pain and heartache long after the initial offense was committed.

The alternative to holding onto this pain is to choose forgiveness. But forgiveness can be very difficult, in part because our anger and hurt lead us to view the other person as our enemy, and to blame them entirely for what we are feeling. A helpful precursor to forgiveness, therefore, can be to cultivate empathy for the person who hurt us. Depending on the nature of the offense, it can help to put ourselves in the other person's shoes. This doesn't mean that we agree with, condone, or validate what they've done. But rather, empathizing allows us to see the other person as a fellow human being, flaws and all, rather than as our adversary.

Once we achieve greater understanding, or even compassion, for the other person, we become more able to forgive. This practice invites you to cultivate the power of empathy and compassion, even towards people who caused you pain previously. As you begin this practice, try starting off with a less painful offense, and work your way up from there.

Instructions: Take a moment and reflect on an ongoing resentment that you carry towards another person. It could be a situation from the distant past, or something more recent. Think about the way in which the person hurt you, and how you felt as a result of their actions. *Notice the emotions that arise when you think about what happened and write them down:*

_____

_____

_____

Next, when you feel ready, try to put yourself in the other person's shoes. Think about what they did, and reflect on why they might have acted the way they did. Try to work from an assumption that this person made a mistake—that they did not act out of pure malice or hate. If it helps, try closing your eyes to get in touch with a sense of compassion towards this person. After some reflection, use the prompts (if applicable) to further guide your process.

1. *How might the person explain what happened, from his or her point of view?*

_____

_____

_____

2. *What was his or her upbringing like?*

_____

_____

_____

3. *How might the person's own past experiences have led him or her to behave in this manner?*

_____

_____

_____

4. *Could the person have meant or intended something different by what he or she said or did?*

_____

_____

_____

5. *Have I ever made a similar mistake?*

_____

_____

_____

6. *Did I play any role in what happened?*

_____

_____

_____

7. *What might a neutral third party say about what occurred?*

_____

_____

_____

8. *How might forgiveness help this person?*

_____

_____

_____

9. *How might forgiveness help me?*

_____

_____

_____

How and why it works: When we find ourselves stuck in a cycle of resentment, we often come to view the person who hurt us as malevolent and out to harm us. While this can certainly be the case, oftentimes there is more nuance to the situation. By cultivating empathy towards this individual, we become better able to gain a new perspective and see the situation from outside our own pain. In fact, some studies show that when we are able to let go of resentment and forgive, areas of our brains associated with empathy and perspective-taking become more active. This practice helps us tap into these states.

Notes/Impressions:

_____

_____

_____

_____

_____

_____

_____

CHAPTER 9

Cultivating Strengths

> *The good life is using your signature strengths every day to produce authentic happiness and abundant gratification.*
>
> —Martin Seligman

> *Compassion and tolerance are not a sign of weakness, but a sign of strength.*
>
> —His Holiness, the Dalai Lama

A Strength-Based Approach to Change

Throughout most of its existence, mental health research and practice has focused almost exclusively on the understanding and treatment of illness. Although this has undoubtedly reduced a great deal of suffering and helped countless individuals, it also misses something important. In short, it misses what is right with people.

One of the key tenets of positive psychology is the belief that it is just as important to learn about people's strengths and gifts as it is to learn about their deficits and shortcomings. A key way in which this has been accomplished is through the study of *personal strengths*. Psychologists Martin Seligman and Chris Peterson, who performed extensive research around the world on this topic, conducted one of the most seminal efforts on this topic. What emerged from their research was the uncovering of 24 distinct "character strengths" that were largely universal, and appreciated cross-culturally as being important to a life well-lived. In the following exercises, you'll be invited to both identify and learn to cultivate your own strengths in several ways.

What Are Strengths?

There have been many definitions of strengths throughout the positive psychology literature, but a concise and effective definition comes from Alex Linley, the founding director for the Centre for Applied Positive Psychology in the United Kingdom. According to Linley, a personal strength can be defined as:

> *A pre-existing capacity for a particular way of behaving, thinking, or feeling that is authentic and energizing to the user, and enables optimal functioning, development, and performance.*

Strengths tend to be stable over time, and help promote optimal performance and functioning in each of us. When we engage our strengths we tend to feel invigorated and revitalized, and are more likely to perform at our best, both psychologically and physically.

Why Cultivate Strengths?

Over the past 15 years or so, there has been a substantial amount of research done on the many benefits of identifying and harnessing our own strengths. Although the following findings are not exhaustive, they provide a sense of how powerful it can be to utilize our strengths on an everyday level.

Individuals who regularly tap into their unique strengths have been found to have higher levels of happiness, along with enhanced levels of life satisfaction. Studies have shown they also have lower levels of depression and anxiety. Among school-age populations, students who regularly engage their strengths and use them on an ongoing basis have higher levels of engagement and performance in the classroom. Similarly, among working adults, the deployment of strengths has been associated with higher levels of performance along with increased job retention. Finally, within relationships, couples that appreciate and encourage the use of their partner's strengths have been found to have higher rates of relationship satisfaction.

The 24 Character Strengths

In the coming pages we will be discussing these strengths in greater depth, but for reference, here is a listing of the 24 strengths identified by Seligman and Peterson:

- Creativity
- Curiosity
- Open-Mindedness
- Love of Learning
- Perspective
- Love
- Kindness
- Social Intelligence
- Bravery

- Persistence
- Integrity
- Vitality
- Forgiveness and Mercy
- Humility and Modesty
- Prudence
- Self-Regulation
- Citizenship
- Leadership

- Fairness
- Appreciation of Beauty and Excellence
- Hope
- Gratitude
- Humor
- Spirituality

Identify Your Strengths

. . . .

Duration: 30-45 minutes

Frequency: One time; but can be repeated if desired

Level of Difficulty: Easy

Overview: The cultivation of personal strengths has been linked to a number of benefits to our bodies and minds, including lower rates of depression and anxiety, and higher rates of happiness and well-being. Although there are many ways to conceptualize this notion of strengths, one remarkable effort to achieve this endeavor was conducted by psychologists Martin Seligman and Christopher Peterson. They scoured the globe, investigating dozens of cultures, reviewing a vast body of philosophical, psychological, and religious works.

Through their research, Seligman and Peterson identified 24 core strengths of character that appeared to be almost universal—in other words, they were valued across a wide range of different cultures and across time. In this practice, you'll be learning about which of these strengths are most present for you so that you can integrate them more into your everyday life.

Instructions: Many of us have heard that it's good to use our strengths towards meaningful goals, but how to actually identify our core strengths can often be a bit more elusive. To remedy this problem, psychologists Martin Seligman and Christopher Peterson conducted research around the world to identify a series of 24 character strengths that appear to be universally desired and valued. These 24 strengths (which fall under six Core Virtues) are listed below:

The 24 Character Strengths identified by Seligman and Peterson, along with their Six Core Virtues:

Virtue I—Wisdom and Knowledge. These strengths entail the acquisition and use of knowledge, for example:

1. Creativity—The ability to think of new or novel ways to do things.
2. Curiosity—Being interested in experience for its own sake.
3. Open-Mindedness—Being able to examine problems from all sides.
4. Love of Learning—Mastering new topics, skills, or bodies of knowledge.
5. Perspective—Providing wise counsel to others.

Virtue II—Humanity. These strengths involve tending to the needs of others, for example:

6. Love—Valuing close relationships with others.
7. Kindness—Doing good deeds for others in the world.
8. Social Intelligence—Having awareness of others' feelings and emotions.

Virtue III—Courage. These strengths involve being able to exercise one's will to accomplish difficult goals, for example:

9. Bravery—Not shrinking from challenges or threats.
10. Integrity—Valuing genuineness, and taking responsibility for one's actions.
11. Persistence—Not giving up easily, and finishing what one starts.
12. Vitality—Approaching life with excitement and energy.

Virtue IV—Justice. These strengths involve valuing fairness and equality, for example:

13. Citizenship—Being able to work well as a member of a group or team.
14. Fairness—Treating others equally.
15. Leadership—Helping others reach greater heights.

Virtue V—Temperance. These strengths involve guarding against excess, for example:

16. Forgiveness and Mercy—Being able to forgive others, and give second chances.
17. Humility and Modesty—Allowing one's accomplishments to speak for themselves.
18. Prudence—Exercising caution and not taking unnecessary risks.
19. Self-Regulation—Being able to manage and regulate one's emotions and actions.

Virtue VI—Transcendence. These strengths involve connecting to larger purposes and meaning, for example:

20. Appreciation of Beauty and Excellence—Appreciating beauty in different areas of life.
21. Gratitude—Having appreciation for the good things in life.
22. Hope—Expecting the best to happen, and working to achieve it.
23. Humor—Finding joy in laughter, and bringing joy to others.
24. Spirituality—Drawing strength from a higher purpose, or greater meaning in life.

In terms of identifying which of these 24 strengths you possess, and to what degree you embody them, there is actually a scientifically-validated way to go about determining this. All you have to do is go online and take the Values in Action (VIA) Survey, which is available for free at www.viacharacter.org. This free, web-based survey was developed to help people identify their core strengths. It takes around 30 to 45 minutes to complete, and has been validated across various populations and samples around the globe. Once you take the test, you'll be provided a rank-order list of your top strengths.

After taking the VIA survey, write your top five strengths according to the test:

1. _____

2. _____

3. _____

4. _____

5. _____

Reflecting on the above, take a moment to consider the following questions.

What was it like to assess my strengths in this way?

_____

_____

_____

Was there anything surprising about the findings?

_____

_____

_____

Do the core strengths identified in the VIA Survey resonate with me?

_____

_____

_____

How do I feel after seeing my strengths outlined in this manner?

_____

_____

_____

How and why it works: Identifying our strengths is the first key step towards harnessing them in the service of bettering our lives. By taking the VIA Survey, we become able to appreciate our strengths and see their role in shaping our lives. Once we've identified these strengths, we can then begin to integrate them more into our everyday activities.

Notes/Impressions:

_____

_____

_____

_____

_____

_____

_____

_____

_____

You at Your Best

· · · · · · · · · · · · · · · · · · ·

Duration: 20 minutes

Frequency: As needed

Level of Difficulty: Moderate

Overview: When you think back on some of the best times of your life, there's a strong likelihood that you were utilizing one or more of your signature strengths during that time period. For example, perhaps you were having great success at work—you may have been utilizing strengths such as *curiosity*, *creativity*, or *persistence*. Conversely, perhaps you were feeling very satisfied with your romantic relationship—you may have been tapping into strengths such as *love*, *kindness*, or *gratitude*. In this practice, you'll be reflecting back on some of the best moments of your life, and learning about which strengths may have enabled you to achieve those sorts of experiences. Doing so can help us learn more about which strengths may help us attain more happiness in our future.

Instructions: Before starting this exercise, take a moment and write down your top five strengths according to the VIA Survey. If you haven't yet done so, take the free online survey at www.viacharacter.org.

1. _____

2. _____

3. _____

4. _____

5. _____

Next, take a moment and reflect back on a time in your life when you felt at your best. This may be a recent memory, or it may be from further back in the past. Close your eyes if it helps, and think back to a time when you felt fulfilled, happy, connected, and satisfied with your life. *Once you've identified this time period, briefly write down some of the memories that surface for you:*

_____

_____

_____

After you've written about this memory, reflect back on your core signature strengths as identified in the VIA Survey. Which of these were present in your memory of being at your best? How did these particular strengths help you achieve this positive moment of your life? What connection do you see between using these strengths and achieving happiness in your life now? *Write any reactions or reflections you have:*

_____

_____

_____

How and why it works: By reflecting on a time when we felt at our best, and then linking this to our signature strengths, we are better able to appreciate the role of our strengths over the course of our lives. This helps not only to make better sense of our past, but also to provide greater direction for our future.

Notes/Impressions:

_____

_____

_____

_____

How You Use Your Strengths

. . . .

Duration: 15 minutes

Frequency: Weekly

Level of Difficulty: Easy/Moderate

Overview: Understanding and using our strengths has been linked to a number of benefits, including improved mental and physical health, along with enhanced work and school performance. However, there are times when we don't even realize that we are in fact tapping into our strengths on an everyday basis. By pausing and reframing things in this light, we begin to feel better about ourselves and become more likely to use these strengths in the future.

Instructions: Take a moment and reflect back over the past week. Consider various parts of your life, from your work to your home life and relationships. For each day, think about the ways in which you used at least one of your signature strengths. For example, perhaps your strength of *kindness* led you to reach out to a loved one who was having a difficult day, or your strength of *persistence* allowed you to succeed at a challenging task at work. Take a moment and consider the many ways in which your strengths manifested themselves over the past week.

For reference and to help jog your memory, write down your top five signature strengths according to the VIA Survey:

1. _____

2. _____

3. _____

4. _____

5. _____

Although this exercise can be done on a weekly basis as described previously, some individuals prefer to do it nightly so that the experiences are fresher in their memory. Feel free to do it whichever way works best for you and your preferences.

Day/Date	Strengths I Used	How I Used This Strength

Once you have completed this practice, take a moment and briefly consider the following questions.

What was it like to do this exercise?

_____

_____

_____

Did reflecting on using my strengths change my perspective in any way?

_____

_____

_____

What can I learn or take from this experience moving forward?

_____

_____

_____

How and why it works: Identifying and tapping into our strengths has been linked to numerous benefits, including improved physical health, enhanced psychological well-being, and stronger performance at work and in school. By reflecting on the past week and identifying ways in which we've utilized our strengths over that time, we become more able to appreciate the role of our strengths in our lives and consider how to harness them further as time goes on.

Notes/Impressions:

_____

_____

_____

_____

_____

_____

_____

Using Your Strengths in New Ways

. . . .

Duration: Variable

Frequency: Daily for one week

Level of Difficulty: Moderate

Overview: Understanding and using our strengths has been linked to a number of benefits, including improved mental and physical health, along with enhanced work and school performance. In working with strengths, it's important that we expand our comfort zone and learn to use our strengths in new, different, and creative ways. Doing so not only increases our happiness, but has also been linked to a higher degree of *flow* states—the experience of being fully immersed in a meaningful task, such that it feels almost as if time has stopped, which is highly connected to lasting well-being. This practice invites you to reflect on your strengths and consider new ways you might cultivate them.

Instructions: Before starting this exercise, take a moment and write down your top five strengths according to the VIA Survey. If you haven't yet done so, take the free online survey at www.viacharacter.org.

1. _____

2. _____

3. _____

4. _____

5. _____

Next, consider the ways in which you might use each strength in a different way. For example, if one of your signature strengths is a love of learning, you might learn one new fact each day, or sign up for an online course. Conversely, if one of your strengths is gratitude, you might create a gratitude journal or go out of your way to express thanks to people in your life each day. Use the following template to guide your process.

Strength #1: _____

How I might use this strength in a new/different way:

_____

_____

_____

Strength #2: _____

How I might use this strength in a new/different way:

_____

_____

_____

Strength #3: _____

How I might use this strength in a new/different way:

_____

_____

_____

Strength #4: _____

How I might use this strength in a new/different way:

_____

_____

_____

Strength #5: _____

How I might use this strength in a new/different way:

_____

_____

_____

Once you've generated some ideas, commit to using your strengths in new ways over the coming week. Each day, choose one of your top strengths to focus on, and use it in a different way than you typically would. *Use the table to track your progress:*

Day/Date	Strength I Used	New/Different Way I Used This Strength

How and why it works: Identifying and using our strengths has been linked to a host of psychological and physical benefits. In particular, using our strengths in new ways has been associated with increased flow states, which is highly connected to happiness and well-being. By using our strengths in new, different, and creative ways, we can take a meaningful step towards lasting well-being.

Notes/Impressions:

_____

_____

_____

_____

_____

_____

_____

_____

Strengths in the Family

. . . .

Duration: Flexible

Frequency: As desired

Level of Difficulty: Moderate

Overview: One great way to foster greater appreciation and understanding within a family is to learn more about various family members' signature strengths. In doing so, we can begin seeing patterns that emerge, and understand which particular strengths are present across different family members, as well as which ones are more unique to each individual family member.

Instructions: Before starting this exercise, take a moment and write down your top five strengths according to the VIA Survey. If you haven't yet done so, take the free online survey at www.viacharacter.org.

1. _____

2. _____

3. _____

4. _____

5. _____

Next, with one or more of your family members, have them take the VIA Survey as well, in order to determine their top strengths. *Once they have done so, write their top strengths:*

1. _____

2. _____

3. _____

4. _____

5. _____

Ideally, you'll begin to include more and more family members in this process. As you do, a nice variation on this exercise is to begin creating an actual family tree, filling in the signature strengths of your different family members. For individuals who may no longer be alive, you can interview those who knew them well and who might shed light on these individuals' areas of strength. *Feel free to use a format similar to this one in creating your family tree of strengths:*

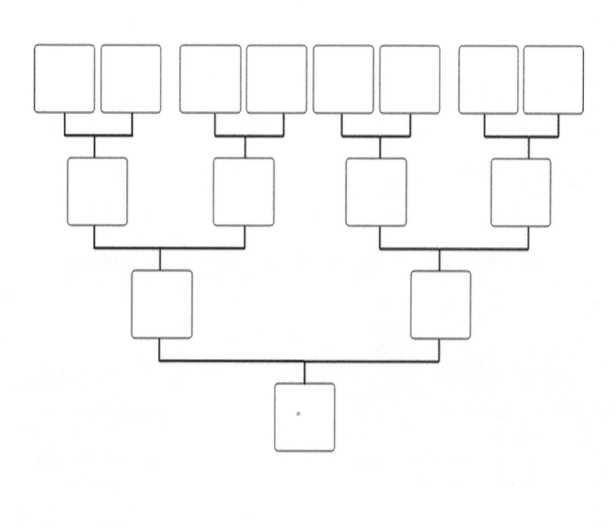

Over time, this practice can help us gain greater understanding and insight into our family members' areas of strength. As you go along, feel free to consider these questions for further reflection.

What patterns emerge when you look at your family's strengths across different individuals, or even different generations?

_____

_____

_____

What strengths are more unique to specific individuals within the family?

_____

_____

_____

When you look at your own strengths, can you trace them back to anyone else in your family who perhaps influenced you?

_____

_____

_____

Does having a greater understanding of your family's strengths give you any insight into behaviors that you previously didn't understand as well?

_____

_____

_____

In what ways might you and your family members use your strengths together to create stronger family connections?

_____

_____

_____

How and why it works: This practice can help us in several ways. First, it provides us with insight into the ways in which various strengths have been present within our family even across generations. It can also lay the groundwork for using our strengths together within our families to foster closer relationships with these individuals, which is another core facet of happiness.

Notes/Impressions:

_____

_____

_____

_____

_____

_____

_____

_____

CHAPTER 10

Savoring the Good

> *Life moves pretty fast. If you don't stop and look around once in awhile, you could miss it.*
> —"Ferris Bueller's Day Off"

> *Everything I need now is here.*
> —Wayne Dyer

What Is Savoring?

We've all been told to "stop and smell the roses" at various points in our lives. But as it turns out, the ability to do just that has been shown to have a tremendous impact on our happiness and well-being, and is closely connected to the practice of *savoring*.

The ability to fully savor and appreciate positive moments in life is a core ingredient of lasting happiness and well-being. In short, savoring refers to the ability to stretch and prolong positive emotional experiences. Rather than simply having a fleeting positive experience, the practice of savoring allows us to draw it out, and get the most of the experience.

Unlike other similar mental states such as mindfulness, savoring can exist across three time spans—the past, the present, and the future. Consider the enjoyment you derive from the simple act of say, eating a piece of chocolate cake. If you were to scarf it down in a matter of seconds, chances are you would experience very little pleasure from the experience. If, on the other hand, imagine that you:

- Anticipate the piece of cake beforehand, imagining how it will taste when you finally take that first bite.
- Slow down and soak up the experience of eating the cake. Notice the smell, the taste, the texture, and so forth, as you eat it.
- Bask in the experience afterwards, taking an extra moment or two to relish how delicious the cake tasted.

We can see in even this somewhat trivial example how much more joy and pleasure can be drawn from the same exact experience when we engage in it in a different way. All our lives contain a mixture of good and bad, pleasant and unpleasant. The simple act of savoring enables us to get the most out of the good aspects of our lives, and makes us much happier over time as we begin to master this skill.

Why Practice Savoring?

Because of our brain's negativity bias, it's easy for us to focus more on negative experiences than positive ones, and for negative parts of our lives to have a greater impact on our mood than positive ones. An antidote for this unfortunate reality is to practice the skill of savoring. In doing so, we become able to draw out and maximize the positive aspects of our lives, allowing them to have a greater impact on our well-being.

Recent research underscores the positive effect that savoring can have on our mental health and well-being. Studies show that individuals who regularly engage in savoring practices tend to be happier and have lower rates of depression and anxiety. They also tend to have higher levels of self-esteem, while also possessing closer interpersonal relationships. Moreover, the practice of savoring has been linked to a number of other positive emotional states associated with happiness, including gratitude, mindfulness, and optimism.

The Savoring Brain

The practice of savoring is closely linked with increased activation in a particular region of our brain called the ventral striatum. This area, which is involved in our brain's "reward center," becomes more activated when we engage in savoring activities. Although some individuals naturally have greater activity in this area, the phenomenon of neuroplasticity underscores the fact that through ongoing practice we can actually see structural changes in the brain over time. Thus, the more we savor, the more these brain regions shift and adapt over time.

On a chemical level, gratitude has been linked to several neurotransmitter systems, including serotonin and dopamine. Serotonin influences a number of bodily functions and is thought to be strongly connected to our moods. Low levels of serotonin are thought by some researchers to be linked to higher rates of depression, and savoring may increase levels of serotonin in our brain. Dopamine, on the other hand, is considered to be a "feel good" neurotransmitter and plays a role in our ability to anticipate rewards and pleasure. Studies suggest that when we engage in savoring, this may also increase levels of dopamine in our brains.

Everyday Savoring

. . . .

Duration: Variable

Frequency: Daily

Level of Difficulty: Easy

Overview: The practice of savoring has been linked to many benefits, including lower rates of depression and anxiety, and higher rates of optimism, joy, happiness, and well-being. However, most of us find that our minds are constantly fixated on stress and worry, and that it's difficult to be fully present with life's joys. There's good reason for this, including our brain's "negativity bias," which refers to the fact that negative experiences have a much more powerful impact on us (and linger with us longer) than positive ones. Savoring is one of the best ways to begin overcoming this negativity bias, and the best place to begin savoring is in our everyday activities that we would normally breeze through on autopilot. This practice invites you to savor one activity each day, and approach it in a new way.

Instructions: In our everyday lives, we often jump from one thing to the next without slowing down or stopping to "smell the roses." Take a moment and reflect on your day-to-day life. Do you notice yourself constantly rushing around, not pausing long enough to appreciate the small stuff? Consider the various activities you engage in each day that, if approached in a different manner, could become sources of greater pleasure. Examples might include:

- Drinking your morning coffee
- Taking a shower
- Cuddling with your dog or cat
- Eating a meal
- Washing the dishes
- Smelling a candle
- Having a moment of connection with a loved one

What sorts of activities do you tend to rush through that might provide an opportunity for savoring?

1. _____
2. _____
3. _____
4. _____
5. _____
6. _____

Next, over the coming week, choose one activity per day to savor in a more robust manner than you usually tend to and record on the form below. When doing so, consider the following guidelines:

- *Use your senses*—consider the various smells, tastes, sights, and textures associated with the experience, and try getting fully in touch with these sensory experiences.
- *Notice your emotions*—when having a pleasant experience, try to really get in touch with the positive emotions that are brought out by it.
- *Share the experience*—another way to fully savor positive experiences is to share them with others.
- *Anticipate the experience*—if it's something that you know is going to happen soon, try spending time anticipating it.
- *Reflect on it afterwards*—instead of just moving on to the next thing, try revisiting the experience even after it's over and reminiscing about what it felt like.

Use the table to track your savoring experiences over the coming week:

Day/Date	Activity That I Savored	How It Felt To Savor This Experience

How and why it works: Slowing down to fully experience the good things in life is an indispensable skill for lasting happiness. All too often we move onto the next thing or fixate on the negative, rather than amplifying and drawing out the positive. Through the simple practice of savoring, we become better able to strengthen and intensify positive experiences, which helps to promote meaningful changes to our happiness and well-being.

Notes/Impressions:

_____

_____

Savoring Through Visualization

. . . .

Duration: 10 minutes

Frequency: Variable/Flexible

Level of Difficulty: Easy

Overview: The practice of savoring has been linked to many benefits, including lower rates of depression and anxiety and higher rates of optimism, joy, happiness, and well-being. At its core, savoring refers to the ability to draw out and maximize positive experiences in our lives. However, many of us find it difficult to "hold onto" good experiences after they're gone. Indeed, many wonderful experiences from the past—weddings, vacations, job promotions, and so forth—do not enter our minds on a regular basis once they've passed. This practice invites you to use the power of visualization to get fully in touch with a past experience of great joy.

Instructions: Take a moment to reflect on some of your favorite memories. Perhaps it was the birth of a child, an incredible travel experience you had, your wedding day, or some other wonderful time in your life. *Choose one of these memories, and briefly write it down:*

_____

_____

_____

_____

_____

Take a moment and respond to the following questions, to get more fully in touch with this memory.

What feelings or emotions do I remember most from this experience?

_____

_____

_____

Who was there? Which people in my life were present for this memory?

_____

_____

_____

What were the sights, smells, tastes, sounds, or textures associated with this joyful memory?

_____

_____

_____

What other small details about this experience made it special for me?

_____

_____

_____

Next, once you've had a chance to get more in touch with this special memory, gently take three slow breaths and close your eyes. For the next few minutes, allow yourself to visualize this positive memory more fully, basking in whatever feelings come from it. If your mind wanders elsewhere, just make note of that, and redirect your awareness back to your memory. In your mind's eye, paint in the small mental details, allowing yourself to become even more immersed in this pleasant memory. After a few minutes, open your eyes and return to the present moment. *Once you've done so, write any brief reactions or observations you had about the experience:*

_____

_____

_____

How and why it works: Visualizing past experiences that were meaningful and joyful for us is one of the most effective ways to practice the powerful skill of savoring. By calling to mind some of these experiences, we can draw them out more fully and re-experience the emotions we felt, which can create a greater sense of both pleasure and meaning.

Notes/Impressions:

_____

_____

_____

_____

_____

_____

_____

_____

Savoring Across Time

. . . .

Duration: Flexible

Frequency: Variable

Level of Difficulty: Variable

Overview: One of the key benefits of savoring is that it allows us to experience positive emotions related to a given event across three cross-sections of time—the past, the present, and the future. In other words, we can derive pleasure or joy from the same exact experience across these three moments in time—first by anticipating the experience, then by fully immersing ourselves in it, and finally by reflecting and reliving the experience. In this practice, you'll be learning to draw out and maximize a positive experience across these three time points.

Instructions: A gift that we can derive from the practice of savoring is the ability to fully maximize pleasant or positive experiences. One of the ways to accomplish this is to think about savoring as existing across three spans of time—the past, the present, and the future. To take a simple example, consider the experience of going on a vacation. Many of us find that in the time leading up to a vacation we are scrambling to tie up any loose ends, driving up our stress in the meantime. Once we're there, we might find ourselves on a beautiful beach or vista, but in our mind, we are replaying various sources of stress and dreading what's to come when we finally must go home. And then finally, once we do return home after our vacation, we so quickly fall back into the daily grind that we derive little if any relaxation and pleasure from our travels after the fact.

Needless to say, this sort of pattern (though not uncommon) is not a great recipe for lasting well-being, happiness, or joy. Consider instead if we were to go about planning for and engaging in our vacation in a different way, as shown on the next page.

Build-up/Anticipation for the trip	Being on vacation	Following vacation
• Look at pictures each night of where you will be traveling. • Plan in an excited but relaxed manner, anticipating the sights and experiences that are to come. • Talk with your traveling companion about what you're most looking forward to.	• Luxuriate in the experiences, fully soaking up the joys and pleasures of the trip. • Be fully present—don't worry too much about snapping the perfect photo, just enjoy the experience. • Cut off technology—don't be glued to your phone. • Don't live in the future—when you notice yourself worrying about returning to "real life," redirect your awareness to the present.	• Talk about your favorite memories from the trip. • Keep a photo album and periodically look through it to relive the trip. • Keep a meaningful souvenir and make sure it's visible. • Create a travel journal, writing down your favorite memories. Read through it from time to time.

As you can see, the same exact experience (going on a vacation in this case) can lead to vastly different emotional outcomes based on how we approach it. By practicing the skill of savoring across time, we can derive substantially more positivity and joy from the good experiences in our lives.

Over the coming week, choose one activity that you'd like to savor across different moments in time. Use the form below to make note of your experience like in the example from above.

Activity or experience that I will savor: _____

Build-up/Anticipation	The Experience Itself	Aftermath/Follow-through

How and why it works: Savoring enables us to get the most "bang for our buck" when it comes to positive experiences. By anticipating future joys, soaking up pleasant moments, and reliving positive memories, we are more able to maximize the good parts of our lives.

Notes/Impressions:

_____

_____

_____

_____

_____

_____

_____

_____

_____

Take a Savoring Walk

. . . .

Duration: 10 minutes

Frequency: Daily for one week

Level of Difficulty: Easy

Overview: Much of the time, we don't pause long enough to appreciate the good things that may be right in front of us in life. We may be stressed, overwhelmed, distracted, or just plain old busy. But whatever the reason, we often find ourselves missing genuine opportunities for pleasant experiences and positive emotions. The practice of savoring enables us to both notice and appreciate positive experiences, and to amplify their effect on our well-being. In this practice you'll be spending a brief bit of time each day going on a "Savoring Walk," in which you'll notice as many sources of joy and positivity as you can.

Instructions: Over the next week, set aside 10-15 minutes per day to go on a "Savoring Walk." Do your walk outside, and keep one primary goal in mind: to notice and experience as many pleasant or positive things in your environment. These could be beautiful sights, soothing sounds, sweet smells—anything that you might normally not take the time to notice and appreciate.

Try setting a timer, so that you can be fully present during the time of your walk. As you notice each positive thing in your environment, really take the time to slow down and soak it up. See if you can be aware of both the sensory and emotional experiences that come up for you. If you can, try to have some variation in terms of where you walk each day as well—the more variation you can find, the more opportunity for new sources of joy and positivity.

How and why it works: As with other savoring practices, the "Savoring Walk" helps us to "stop and smell the roses" and appreciate the positive things that surround us every day. By pausing, noticing, and appreciating these things, we can drastically enhance our happiness and well-being over time. Instead of allowing these sources of joy to slip through our fingertips and out of our conscious awareness, we can maximize their impact on our mood and our health.

Notes/Impressions:

_____

_____

_____

_____

_____

_____

_____

_____

Taking in the Good

. . . .

Duration: Under one minute

Frequency: Daily—as often as possible

Level of Difficulty: Easy

Overview: Because of our brain's "negativity bias," we are hardwired to notice threats in our lives, and to focus on the negative far more than the positive. When we do have negative experiences, they stick with us much more intensely, even on a neuronal and physiological level. Conversely, positive experiences often roll off us, like water off a duck. The neuropsychologist Rick Hanson has thusly described our brains as being like "Teflon for good, and Velcro for bad."

The good news is that we can, over time, learn to rewire our brains for positivity. But in order to do that, we must train our mind to seek out and relish positive micro-moments of joy, tranquility, and happiness in our lives. Hanson refers to this process as "Taking in the Good"—in other words, simply noticing and savoring positive experiences, and allowing them to sink into your body and mind.

Whenever positive experiences occur in our lives, or when we notice good things around us, it's important that we take a moment and "take in" this source of joy and happiness. This practice invites you to "Take in the Good," which is thought to be one of the most effective ways to change our brains over time through neuroplasticity.

Instructions: Over the coming week, when you experience something good, or have a moment of connection, allow an extra bit of time to fully "take in" this positive experience rather than simply rushing off to the next thing. Use the four steps to enable yourself to fully maximize the positive things in your life:

1. Notice something good in your day-to-day life. This can be a pleasant experience, a positive interaction with a loved one, a moment of kindness that you witness, noticing a beautiful sunset, or enjoying a delicious meal. Whatever it is, take a moment to fully notice this good thing.
2. Allow this positive experience to register, in both your body and mind. Notice what emotions come up for you, and how it feels in your body.
3. Let the experience linger in both your mind and body a bit longer, rather than simply moving onto something else. Take an extra 30 seconds or so to allow the feelings to sit with you, and envision these positive emotions washing over you.

4. Later, revisit and relive this positive experience. You can write about it, share it with someone else, or simply take a few extra moments to envision it and savor it later that day. Doing this step helps to further encode the event in your neural circuitry.

How and why it works: Recent research in neuroscience suggests that allowing even 30 seconds of savoring pleasant experiences can help strengthen neural firing and further encode these things in our memories. This is in direct contrast to how we often may experience something pleasant, only to "put it out of sight and out of mind" quickly thereafter. When we learn to take in the good more regularly and on an ongoing basis, we can begin to maximize the positive experiences in our lives and further create a foundation for happiness.

Notes/Impressions:

_____

_____

_____

_____

_____

_____

_____

CHAPTER 11

Health and Happiness

> *The Groundwork of all Happiness is health.*
>
> —Leigh Hunt

> *Happiness lies, first of all, in health.*
>
> —George William Curtis

Health and Happiness

When we're stressed, our health is often the first thing we neglect. We eat less healthy foods, we stop exercising, and we sleep poorly. Oftentimes, we tell ourselves that we'll get back on track in these areas once we feel better. "I'll start exercising when I'm less stressed," we might say. Or "I'll eat healthier when I'm feeling less depressed." But these sorts of statements miss the simple but crucial point: Taking care of our health and bodies is one of the most effective paths towards happiness and well-being.

Caring for our body can mean many different things, but for the purposes of narrowing our scope, we'll focus on three core ways we can achieve this goal:

- *Exercise*—even modest increases in activity level have been shown to have powerful effects on our psychological well-being.
- *Sleep*—inadequate sleep has been linked to negative outcomes for both our physical and mental health. Improving our sleep can vastly improve our health in these areas.
- *Food*—eating balanced meals, and particularly integrating specific mind-boosting nutrients, can enhance our happiness and well-being.

Why Focus on Our Health?

Recent research has shed light on the link between our mind and our body, and the ways in which our health impacts our mood, and vice versa. Each of the three domains listed above (exercise, sleep, and food) have been found to have specific benefits to our physical and mental health.

Exercise

Numerous studies have shown that exercise has been found to be one of the most effective ways to reduce stress. It has even been found to be effective in the treatment of depression, with one well-known study finding that exercise was equally as effective as antidepressant medications in the treatment of moderate depression. Part of the reason for this may be due to the fact that exercise is thought to increase both serotonin and dopamine in our brains—two of the neurotransmitter systems often targeted by medications.

Moderate exercise has also been shown to decrease levels of cortisol, a stress hormone that over the long-run can weaken our immune system and increase chronic illnesses, as well as reducing chronic inflammation in our bodies. On a brain-based level, exercise has been linked to increased levels of brain-derived neurotrophic factor (BDNF), a protein that helps to maintain healthy neurons and create new ones. Best of all? Even modest increases in our exercise habits can make tremendous changes in our lives.

Sleep

Sleep is inversely correlated with a number of mental health problems, including anxiety, stress, bipolar disorder, and depression (though some people with depression have the opposite problem—sleeping excessively). This is particularly unfortunate since improving sleep is a simple yet effective way to improve these sorts of problems. Worse yet, some studies show that the average American is chronically under-sleeping by at least one hour per night. This sort of sleep deficit wreaks havoc on our health and our mood, as well as our productivity and mental clarity. Even a marginal improvement to our sleep can yield powerful benefits to our psychological well-being, and help to enhance our happiness.

Food

It makes sense that what we put in our bodies has a strong impact on our physical and mental health. But recent research has shed light on some of the specific ways in which our diet affects our psychological well-being and happiness. Although this is a broad area of research, we'll be exploring two specific ways that we can foster happiness and well-being through changes in how we eat: by eating more foods that are anti-inflammatory, as well as by eating specific foods that have nutrients linked to improved mental health.

Get Moving

. . . .

Duration: 20 minutes

Frequency: Four times per week initially

Level of Difficulty: Moderate

Overview: It may seem obvious that engaging in physical exercise would be good for our mental health and happiness, but recent research has shed light on just how widespread these benefits can be. As it turns out, exercise has been found to reduce stress and depression, while increasing happiness, across numerous studies. Best of all, significant benefits can come from as little as 20 minutes of aerobic exercise, several days per week. What constitutes aerobic exercise? The formula is simple:

- Anything that brings your heart rate up to 60-90% of your max heart rate
- Your max heart rate can be calculated by subtracting your age from 220

Despite the fact that we all know intuitively (and have heard it countless times) that exercise is good for our mental health, it is often one of the first things that we neglect when we become stressed or overwhelmed in life. Rather than wait until things settle down before we recommit to our exercise practice, it's imperative that we "put the cart before the horse," so to speak. In other words, prioritizing physical exercise can actually help significantly when it comes to feeling stressed and overwhelmed, not to mention the countless benefits it can offer to our physical and mental health.

In this practice, you're invited to begin experiencing first-hand the benefits of physical exercise to your well-being. Remember, don't worry about turning your life upside-down and spending countless hours at the gym. Feel free to start slow, and work your way up from there.

Instructions: Modest physical exercise has been associated with many benefits to both our physical and emotional health. Indeed, individuals who engage in regular exercise have lower rates of depression and anxiety, along with higher rates of happiness and well-being. Moreover, there are countless physical health benefits to exercise, impacting nearly every part of our body, including our brain health.

When you're considering starting an exercise regimen, remember to allow yourself to start small and make it sustainable. Consider the following when thinking about what sorts of physical activities you'd like to integrate into your life:

- What does your schedule look like? What time of day might be available for you to engage in exercise?
- What are your particular goals for fitness? Would you like to lose weight, gain strength, improve your cardiovascular fitness?
- Are you someone who likes to exercise in a more structured setting, like a gym? Or do you prefer to be outdoors?

With those questions in mind, list a few possible exercise ideas that might appeal to you:

1. _____

2. _____

3. _____

4. _____

5. _____

Once you've come up with a few, use the upcoming week to experiment and try some of them out. Make it a priority, and carve out time in your schedule to engage in some sort of physical activity four or more days in the upcoming week. After each activity, make note of how you feel both physically and emotionally as a result of the activity. *Use the table to keep track of your progress:*

Date	Exercise I Engaged In (Activity, Duration, Etc.)	How I Felt Afterwards (Physically, Emotionally)

How and why it works: Physical exercise helps us in countless ways in terms of our physical and mental health. First and foremost, there are direct physiological benefits to exercise, including reduced stress hormones in the body, increased blood flow in the brain, and increased brain-derived neurotrophic factor (BDNF), which helps with brain cell generation. These changes help explain why exercise is such a great stress reliever and can help with everything from mood to concentration.

Beyond this, exercise can also help a great deal in terms of self-esteem, and creating a sense of control and mastery in our lives. There is even evidence that exercise helps us to create more flow experiences in our lives—the state of total absorption that is highly linked to happiness.

Notes/Impressions:

_____

_____

_____

_____

_____

_____

_____

Fostering Healthy Sleep Habits

• •

Duration: Variable

Frequency: Nightly

Level of Difficulty: Moderate

Overview: Getting a good night's sleep is crucial to our physical and mental health. Unfortunately for many of us, some studies show that the average American under-sleeps by as much as one hour per night. There is no magic number to the exact amount of sleep we all need as individuals; indeed, there is person-to-person variability, and the amount of sleep we need changes throughout our lifespans. Nonetheless, if you find yourself tired throughout the day, feeling sluggish, and lacking mental clarity, chances are you're not sleeping adequately.

There are a number of medical issues that can contribute to sleep problems, including things like chronic pain and sleep apnea. Those are beyond the scope of this book, and readers are encouraged to follow up with their health professionals about these sorts of issues. But for many people, sleep problems come as a result of poor habits related to sleep, and this practice is designed to address some of these common issues.

Instructions: Reflect for a moment on how you've been sleeping of late. Do you wake up feeling well rested and recharged for the coming day? Or do you find yourself feeling sluggish and fatigued? Consider how much sleep you tend to get on average each night, and whether this is adequate for your needs (for reference, visiting https://sleepfoundation.org can provide you with a ballpark estimate of your sleep needs at various stages of life).

If you find yourself struggling with sleep, take a moment and write down some of the effects of poor sleep that you've experienced:

_____

_____

_____

Next, look over the following list of behavioral sleep strategies that can either help or hinder our ability to get a good night's sleep. You'll notice that it's broken down into a list of "do's" and "don'ts." *Make note of which ones you're doing well on, as well as the ones that might be sabotaging your ability to sleep:*

Do's—These habits help foster a good night's sleep	Don'ts—These may hurt your ability to sleep well at night
• Keep a regular sleep/wake schedule • Exercise regularly—but not within 3 hours of bedtime • Keep a comfortable sleep environment—consider temperature, bedding, lighting, etc. • Shut off all bright screens—including phones and televisions—at least 1 hour before bedtime • Establish a relaxing pre-bedtime routine—this can include things like taking a warm bath, listening to soft music, or drinking chamomile tea • Use your bed only for sleep or sex	• Take daytime naps—these can interfere with your ability to sleep well at night • Use stimulants such as caffeine or nicotine (especially within 6 hours of bedtime) • Go to bed too hungry or too full • Exercise vigorously within 3 hours of bedtime • Drink alcohol—especially within 3 hours of bedtime • Stay in bed when you can't sleep—if you cannot fall asleep within 30 minutes, get out of bed and try a low-stimulation activity (such as reading in low light) • Watch TV in bed, eat in bed, talk on the phone in bed—these can make it harder to sleep at night • Watch the clock

How and why it works: Sleep is crucial to our well-being—there's a reason after all that we spend roughly one-third of our lives sleeping. Deficient sleep has been linked to a number of physical health problems including heart disease, high blood pressure, stroke, and diabetes, along with a host of mental health issues including depression and anxiety. Although some sleep problems are linked to more serious health problems, much of the time simple behavioral and habit changes can lead to lasting positive improvements when it comes to our sleep.

Notes/Impressions:

_____

_____

_____

_____

_____

Relaxing Your Muscles

· ·

Duration: 15-20 minutes

Frequency: As needed

Level of Difficulty: Easy/Moderate

Overview: Without even realizing it, many of us habitually hold tension in our bodies throughout the day. For some of us it's our shoulders, while for others it may be our back or neck. Many individuals struggling with stress and anxiety hold so much tension throughout the day that they don't recognize what it's like for their bodies to feel relaxed. Regardless, our bodies tends to "store" stress and tension—this exercise is designed to help you release this tension and promote relaxation.

This practice is called the "Progressive Muscle Relaxation," and it teaches you to relax the muscles throughout your body in a two-step process. First, we actually tense a particular group of muscles, such as your shoulders or forearms. Then, we release the tension and allow the feeling of relaxation to spread throughout the area. Progressive Muscle Relaxation (PMR) has been shown to be helpful in a number of areas, including reducing physical stress, lowering anxiety, and even helping with conditions like insomnia and chronic pain.

Be mindful not to injure yourself in this practice. If you have a health condition, or feel sharp shooting pains at any point, consult with your physician.

Instructions: When you practice Progressive Muscle Relaxation (PMR), there are essentially two main steps:

* First, you apply muscle tension to a particular part of your body. In doing so, take a deep and slow breath, while squeezing your muscles in that area tightly for around five to seven seconds. You want to really feel the tension in your muscles, but don't push yourself to the point of pain.

* Next, as you exhale, release the tension that you've been holding in that muscle area. When you do so, allow the tension to rapidly be released as you exhale (in around five seconds), and then allow yourself to remain in this relaxed and loose state for another 10-15 seconds thereafter. Take your time to deliberately focus on the difference between the sensation of being tense and being relaxed, as this is one of the most important parts of this practice.

This basic two-step process (inhale and tensing, followed by exhale and releasing) is then repeated across a number of core muscle groups. At first this practice can feel a bit uncomfortable, and it can take practice to learn and feel the difference between relaxation and tension in our bodies. But over time it becomes more of a habit, and can lead to great rewards for our health and happiness. In beginning your practice, feel free to use this script to help get you started:

Begin by setting aside roughly 15 minutes. Be sure that you are in a quiet place where you won't be disturbed, and can do this exercise without interruption. Wear loose, comfortable clothing that you can move around in, and take off your shoes. Find a quiet place to sit, and when you're ready, close your eyes. Take five slow, deep breaths before getting started.

Allow yourself to focus only on your body. You may notice your mind wandering or your thoughts drifting, and that's totally normal. Simply return your attention each time to this practice. Slow your breath down ever so slightly, breathing deeply through your abdomen. Observe your stomach rising and falling with each breath, and feel your lungs filling with air.

As you inhale, remember to tense your muscle group and hold it for five to seven seconds. When you exhale, release the tension, visualizing it leaving your body. Remember to keep breathing, and not hold your breath.

When you're ready, begin by tightening the muscles in your forehead, raising your eyebrows as high as you're able to. Hold for five seconds, feeling the tension spread throughout your forehead. And then exhale, rapidly releasing the tension. Pause for another 10 seconds to fully allow the feeling of relaxation to spread in your face.

Next, smile widely, feeling the tension spread throughout your cheeks and mouth. Hold for five seconds, feeling the tension continue to spread. And then release, feeling the tension drain from your face. Pause for another 10 seconds to feel the relaxation spread more fully throughout your face.

Now shifting your focus to your eyes, tighten your eye muscles by squinting your eyes shut, feeling the tension spread throughout your eyes. After five seconds, rapidly release the tension, feeling the tension drain and relaxation spread throughout your face. Pause for another 10 seconds to feel the relaxation spread more fully.

Next, gently lean your head back, looking above you to the ceiling. Hold the pose, feeling the tension spread through your neck. After five seconds, rapidly release the tension, bringing your head back down. Pause for another 10 seconds, feeling the relaxation spread throughout your neck and the back of your head.

Now, shifting your awareness down to your hands, clench your fists tightly until you feel the tension spread throughout your hands and fist. After five seconds, release and feel the tension melt away and the relaxation spread throughout your hands. Pause for another 10 seconds, continuing to feel the relaxation in your hands.

Next, flex your biceps, and feel the tension spread throughout your arms. Hold for five seconds, and then release and notice the feelings of relaxation spread throughout your arms. Continue to breathe, slowly in and slowly out, feeling more and more relaxation come over your body.

Next, lift your shoulders upward, as if trying to touch your ears with them. Hold for five seconds, feeling the tension continuing to spread, and then release, noticing the tension melt away and the relaxation spreading through your shoulders. Pause for 10 more seconds, continuing to feel the relaxation and limpness spreading throughout your shoulders and body.

Now, create tension in your upper back as you pull your shoulders backward, as if trying to make your shoulder blades touch. Feel the tension spread in this area, holding for five seconds. Then release, and notice the relaxation spread rapidly. Pause for 10 more seconds, and continue to notice the feeling of relaxation spread throughout this area.

Next, create tightness and tension in your chest by taking a full, deep inhale. Breathe in as deep as you can, holding for five seconds, and then exhale steadily, releasing all the tension in your chest. Pause for 10 seconds, feeling the relaxation spread throughout your chest.

Now shift the awareness to your stomach, and tighten the muscles in your stomach by sucking in your breath and holding it. Allow the tension to build, and after five seconds, release the tension. Pause for 10 seconds, and allow your stomach to feel fully relaxed.

Next, arch your lower back and hold for five seconds, feeling the tension spread in this area. Then release, and feel the tension melt away. Pause for 10 seconds, and allow the feelings of relaxation to spread throughout your upper body. Notice your head, neck, shoulders, arms, and back, all feeling relaxed and loose.

Now tighten the muscles in your buttocks, holding for five seconds and feeling the tension spread. Then release, and feel the tension melt away. Pause another 10 seconds to allow the feelings of relaxation to spread.

Next, tighten your thigh muscles by pressing your knees together, as if trying to hold something between your legs. Continue to hold for five seconds, noticing the tension spread in this area, then release, feeling the relaxation kick in and begin to spread. Pause another 10 seconds to fully soak up these feelings of relaxation.

Next, extend your legs and pull your toes upwards towards your face, feeling the tension spread throughout your calves. Hold for five seconds, really feeling the tension begin to spread. And then release the tension away, pausing another 10 seconds to fully experience the sensation of relaxation.

Now, extend your legs once more, this time tilting your toes down towards the floor. Hold for five seconds, and notice the tension begin to spread. Then release, feeling the tension melt away. Pause 10 seconds to fully feel this relaxation spread throughout your legs.

Continue to breathe, and allow the feelings of relaxation to continue spreading throughout your body. Notice the feelings of looseness in your muscles, now feeling fully relaxed and peaceful.

How and why it works: The "Progressive Muscle Relaxation" is a powerful exercise that can promote deep feelings of tranquility and relaxation throughout our bodies. Since we often don't even realize how much tension we may be holding in our bodies, this practice helps us to recognize the difference between tension and relaxation, and helps promote the relaxation response when practiced. It's a great practice not only for promoting feelings of calm, but also for other issues including chronic pain and migraine headaches.

Notes/Impressions:

_____

_____

_____

_____

_____

_____

_____

_____

_____

_____

A Meditation for Sleep

. . . .

Duration: 10-15 minutes

Frequency: Nightly before bed

Level of Difficulty: Easy/Moderate

Overview: Getting a good night's sleep is crucial to our physical and mental health. Unfortunately for many of us, some studies show that the average American under-sleeps by as much as one hour per night. There is no magic number to the exact amount of sleep we all need as individuals; there is person-to-person variability, and the amount of sleep we need changes throughout our lifespans. Nonetheless, if you find yourself tired throughout the day, feeling sluggish, and lacking mental clarity, chances are you're not sleeping adequately.

There are a number of medical issues that can contribute to sleep problems, including things like chronic pain and sleep apnea. Those are beyond the scope of this book, and readers are encouraged to follow up with their health professionals around these sorts of issues. But for many people, sleep problems come as a result of not being properly relaxed heading into bedtime. This simple meditation helps foster feelings of relaxation, in order to promote a good night's sleep.

Instructions: Spend about 10-15 minutes practicing this meditation to help you unwind and relax before bed each night. To help it be even more effective, combine this practice with healthy sleep habits like the ones described earlier in this section. Some people find it helpful to record this script in their own voice, or have a loved one record it whose voice they find particularly soothing.

Begin by lying down comfortably in your bed, and taking a few slow, even, soothing breaths. Close your eyes, and allow your breath to slow down ever so slightly, particularly on your exhale. With each passing breath, become more aware of the feeling of your body in the bed, and notice any sensations that are present in your body right now. For example, you might notice the temperature, any muscle tension or strain, any itchiness, and so forth.

Continue to become more aware of all these sensations, but be mindful not to judge them—simply notice your experiences as you continue to breathe. With each passing breath, notice yourself feeling ever so slightly more relaxed.

Once your breath is sufficiently slowed and you're starting to feel relaxed, begin gently scanning your body, envisioning the relaxation beginning to spread. Start at your extremities—the tips of your toes and fingers—and work your way up slowly from there. With each passing breath, bring awareness to these parts of your body, feeling the relaxation spread. From your toes and fingers, shift gently to your wrists and ankles, continuing to feel the relaxation spread.

When you notice judgments, thoughts, or reactions arise, simply notice these without trying to push them away. Redirect your awareness each time to your breathing, and to the feeling of relaxation spreading throughout your body. From your wrists and ankles, move up to your forearms and lower legs. From there, move up to your knees and elbows, gradually moving closer to your heart with each stage. Feel your arms relax, your legs, your back, and so forth. If you encounter lingering tension in any area in particular, take an extra moment to breathe and relax.

Once you've worked your way through your body, scan once more to see if any areas of lingering tension remain. You can also go back and scan your body once more if you need to. Once you feel fully relaxed, allow yourself to gently fall into sleep.

How and why it works: Sleep is crucial to our well-being—there's a reason after all that we spend roughly one-third of our lives sleeping. Deficient sleep has been linked to a number of physical health problems including heart disease, high blood pressure, stroke, and diabetes, along with a host of mental health issues including depression and anxiety. Much of the time, we struggle to sleep because we haven't properly promoted ample relaxation heading into bedtime. Combined with healthy sleep habits, this sleep meditation can help promote deep feelings of relaxation and tranquility, laying the groundwork for a healthy night's sleep.

Notes/Impressions:

_____

_____

_____

_____

_____

_____

Nutrients for Happiness

· ·

Duration: N/A

Frequency: Daily

Level of Difficulty: Easy/Moderate

Overview: We've all heard it said that the way we eat impacts how we feel. Although it makes intuitive sense that the foods we put in our bodies affect our mood, recent research has shed light over some of the more specific effects of food on our mental health and well-being. Beyond simply eating a balanced diet, eating plenty of fruits and vegetables, and reducing processed foods, there are a set of specific nutrients that have been linked to psychological well-being and even brain health. In this practice, you're invited to integrate a set of six specific nutrients that have been found to contain unique benefits to our mental health.

Instructions: Even small changes to our diet can yield significant benefits to both our physical and psychological well-being. Having a healthy diet means that we eat for balance, reduce processed foods, cut down on sugar, and eat several servings of fruits and vegetables each day. But in addition to these more general guidelines, recent research has shed light on a series of specific nutrients that can benefit our mental health and even promote healthy brain functioning. In the following table you will see a list of these nutrients, a brief overview of their specific benefits, along with some foods that contain ample volumes of these nutrients.

Nutrient	Impact on Mental Health and Well-Being	Foods That Contain This Nutrient
Omega 3s	Combats depression Reduces fatigue Stabilizes mood swings	Salmon Spinach Herring
Magnesium	Reduces stress Lessens fatigue Helps treatment-resistant depression (TRD)	Spinach Almonds Cashews Edamame
Vitamin D	Fights depression Improves brain cell regeneration	Eggs Salmon Swordfish Milk

Nutrient	Impact on Mental Health and Well-Being	Foods That Contain This Nutrient
Zinc	Improves depression	Beef Peanuts Kidney Beans Pumpkin Seeds
Chromium	Increases serotonin and dopamine May reduce depressive symptoms	Turkey Broccoli Grapefruit
Folate	Helps with brain cell regeneration	Spinach Avocado Brussels Sprouts

In the coming weeks, try to slowly integrate some of these nutrients into your regular diet. Even small changes can go a long way, so it's okay to start small. But foods such as the ones listed above can form the foundation of our happiness, helping to improve our mood and lower stress. As you begin to make these changes, see if you are able to notice any changes when it comes to your mood, stress levels, and mental clarity. And as always, consult with a nutritionist or your personal physician if you have any specific health conditions.

How and why it works: The foods we eat can have a significant impact on our psychological well-being. The specific nutrients outlined in this practice have been shown to have unique benefits to our psychological health and emotional well-being. By integrating them into our regular diet, we can reduce stress, achieve higher levels of well-being, and improve our brain health.

Notes/Impressions:

_____

_____

_____

_____

_____

_____

Relaxing Through Our Breath

. . . .

Duration: 1-5 minutes

Frequency: As needed

Level of Difficulty: Easy

Overview: Breathing is something that we all do each and every day, from the moment we're born, yet much of the time it occurs outside of our conscious awareness, and happens automatically. Although we've probably all been told that we should "relax and take a deep breath" during times of stress, recent research has shed light on the powerful impact that our breathing has on our psychological well-being. Indeed, slowing our breath can help reduce feelings of stress and promote calmness and tranquility.

Our breath and our emotions are deeply intertwined—when we experience certain emotions, it changes the way we breathe. We've probably all experienced this first-hand—when we're stressed or anxious, we take shallow, rapid breaths. Conversely, when we feel calm and at ease, our breathing tends to be slower and deeper. But what we often don't realize, particularly in difficult moments, is that the direction of this relationship works both ways. In other words, when we consciously and deliberately slow our breath down and deepen it, we are able to promote relaxation and calmness through our entire body.

One of the reasons why slow breathing can have such an impact on our body is that it helps activate our vagus nerve, which helps slow down our sympathetic nervous system (linked to our fight-or-flight response) and activates our parasympathetic nervous system (which promotes feelings of calm and relaxation). Exhalations in particular help slow our heart rate—the more that we slow down our out-breath, the calmer we become.

Instructions: Over the coming week, set aside a few minutes each day to focus on your breathing and to practice slowing your breath down. Our breath is with us each moment of every day, but often exists outside our conscious awareness, and yet deliberately breathing in a slower manner (particularly on our exhale) has been linked to a host of benefits—most notably reduced stress and increased calmness.

Begin by setting aside a few minutes of each day (set an alarm or reminder if it helps) to focus on your breath. First notice how you are breathing—is your breath slow and steady, or is it shallow or choppy? Next, close your eyes, and allow your breath to slow down ever so slightly, in particular slowing down as you exhale. Allow your exhales to be slightly longer than your inhales. Find the timing that works for

- Set aside time to "replay" the experience in your mind, allowing the feelings of calm and relaxation to be relived.
- Talk it over—studies show that opening up about our emotional experience and sharing good memories helps us to capitalize on these positive experiences.
- Share the moment—try linking up with someone else to share these experiences in nature.
- Tap into feelings of awe—while out in nature, take a moment to really soak up the vastness of the experience, and the feeling of awe that it can evoke.

How and why it works: For many years, various thinkers, writers, and philosophers have espoused the benefits of being in nature. As it turns out these were not just pleasant sentiments, but in fact held great truth that modern science is only beginning to unlock. Recent research has discovered some of the many benefits to our minds and bodies that stem from being around nature. By increasing our time spent in nature and around green spaces, we can promote feelings of calmness and joy in our lives.

Notes/Impressions:

_____

_____

_____

_____

_____

_____

_____

Bibliography

· · · · · · · · · · · · ·

Abel, E. L., & Kruger, M. L. (2010). Smile intensity in photographs predicts longevity. *Psychological Science, 21*, 542-544.

Algoe, S. (2010). It's the little things: Everyday gratitude as a booster shot for romantic relationships. *Personal Relationships, 17(2)*, 217-233.

Boehm, J. & Kubzansky, L. (2012). The heart's content: The association between positive psychological well-being and cardiovascular health. *Psychological Bulletin, 138*, 665-691.

Dane, E., & Brummel, B.J. (2013). Examining workplace mindfulness and its relations to job performance and turnover intention. *Human Relations*, Sage Journals.

Danner, D., & Snowdon, D. (2001). Positive emotions in early life and longevity: Findings from the nun study. *Journal of Personality and Social Psychology, 80*, 804-813.

Diener, E. (1999). Subjective well-being: Three decades of progress. *Psychological Bulletin*, 125, 276-302

Diener, E. (2000). Subjective well-being: The science of happiness and a proposal for a national index. *American Psychologist, 55*, 34-43.

Diener, E., & Biswas-Diener, R. (2008). *Happiness: Unlocking the mysteries of psychological wealth*. Oxford: Blackwell Publishing.

Dunn, E.W. (2008). Spending money on others promotes happiness. *Science, 319* (5870): 1687-1688.

Emmons, R. (2007). *Thanks! How practicing gratitude can make you happier*. New York: Houghton Mifflin Company.

Emmons R.A., & McCullough, M.E. (2003). Counting blessings versus burdens: An experimental investigation of gratitude and subjective well-being in daily life. *Journal of Personality and Social Psychology, 84*, 377-389.

Emmons, R.A., & Shelton, C.M. (2002). Gratitude and the science of positive psychology. In Snyder, C.R., & Lopez, S.J. (eds.). *Handbook of Positive Psychology*, 459-471. Oxford: Oxford University Press.

Fredrickson, B. (2009). *Positivity: Top-notch research reveals the 3 to 1 ratio that will change your life*. Harmony Press.

Gable, E. L., Reis, H. T., Impett, E. A., & Asher, E. R. (2004). Capitalizing on daily positive events. *Journal of Personality and Social Psychology, 87*.

Gilbert, D. (2006). *Stumbling on happiness*. New York: Knopf.

Hanson, R. (2009). *Buddha's brain: The practical neuroscience of happiness, love, and wisdom*. Oakland: New Harbinger Publications.

Holt-Lunstad, J. (2010). Social relationships and mortality risk: A meta-analytic review. *PLoS Medicine, 7*.

Keng, S. (2011). Effects of mindfulness on psychological health: A review of empirical studies. *Clinical Psychology Review, 31*, 1041-1056.

Killingsworth, M., & Gilbert, D. (2010). A wandering mind is an unhappy mind. *Science, 330*, 932.

King, L.A. (2001). The health benefits of writing about life goals. *Personality and Social Psychology Bulletin, 27*, 798-807.

King, L., & Miner, K. (2000). Writing about the perceived benefits of traumatic events: Implications for physical health. *Personality and Social Psychology Bulletin, 26*, 220-230.

Koo, M., Algoe, S., Wilson, T., & Gilbert, D. (2008). It's a wonderful life: Mentally subtracting positive events improves people's affective states, contrary to their affective forecasts. *Journal of Personality and Social Psychology, 95*, 1217-1224.

Lieberman, M. (2013). *Social: Why our brains are wired to connect*. Crown Publishing

Luskin, F. (2002). *Forgive for good: A proven prescription for health and happiness*. New York: Harper Collins.

Lyubomirsky, S. (2007). *The how of happiness: A new approach to getting the life you want*. New York: Penguin Books

Lyubomirsky, S., King, L., & Diener, E. (2005). The benefits of frequent positive affect: Does happiness lead to success? *Psychological Bulletin, 131*, 803-855.

Neff, K. (2009). Self compassion. In Leary, M., & Hoyle, R. (ed.), *Handbook of individual differences in social behavior*. New York: Guilford Press.

Neff, K. (2011). *Self-Compassion: The Proven Power of Being Kind to Yourself*. William Morrow.

Oman, D., Thoresen, C.E., & McMahon, K. (1999). Volunteerism and mortality among the community-dwelling elderly. *Journal of Health Psychology, 4*(3).

Ortake, K. (2006). Happy people become happier through kindness: A counting kindnesses intervention. *Journal of Happiness Studies, 7*, 361-375.

Seligman, M.E.P. (2002). *Authentic happiness*. New York: Free Press.

Seligman, M.E.P. (2006). *Learned optimism*. Vintage Press.

Seligman, M.E.P., Rashid, T., & Parks, A.C. (2006). Positive psychotherapy. *American Psychologist, 61*, 774-788.

Vaillant, G. (2012). Triumphs of experience: The men of the Harvard grant study. Belknap Press.